**The Businessman's
Complete Checklist**

The Businessman's Complete Checklist

W. C. Shaw & G. J. Day

BUSINESS BOOKS
COMMUNICA - EUROPA

First published 1978
© Business Books Ltd.

No part of this publication may be reproduced or transmitted in any form without written permission from the publishers.

ISBN 0 220 66359 9

Typeset by TNR Productions W1
Printed and bound in Great Britain
by W & J Mackay Limited, Chatham
for Business Books Ltd., 24 Highbury Crescent,
London N5

Contents

DISTRIBUTION AND STORAGE

1. Warehouse control procedures
2. Warehouse operating efficiency
3. Distribution, packaging and routing
4. Physical distribution facilities audit
5. Physical distribution facilities
6. Physical distribution system and design
7. Transport
8. New warehouse building
9. Negotiations
10. Vehicle security procedures

PERSONNEL

1. Personnel activities
2. Role of the personnel function
3. Personnel managers' duties
4. Salary policies
5. Salary administration
6. Basic features of a salary structure
7. Fixed v Variable system of rewards
8. Profit sharing schemes
9. Bonus scheme criteria
10. Share ownership schemes
11. Need for management development and manpower planning
12. Elements of a manpower plan
13. Manpower planning
14. Recruitment and selection within a manpower plan
15. Training within a manpower plan
16. Managing the high flier
17. Factors affecting work force size
18. Basic reasons for leaving
19. Job specifications
20. Job specification preparation
21. Job evaluation/performance assessment
22. Choice of job evaluation scheme
23. Pension schemes
24. Changing a pension scheme

FINANCE AND ACCOUNTING

1. Sources of finance
2. Balance sheet structure
3. Balance sheet classifications
4. Understanding the balance sheet and profit and loss account
5. Principal management ratios
6. Principal variations of return on capital concept
7. Return on capital ratio
8. Gearing, cash and working capital ratios
9. Return on capital ratios by product
10. Manufacturing ratios
11. Machine capacity ratios
12. Labour utilisation ratios
13. Priority ratios for Chief Executive
14. Financial objectives of management in ratio terms
15. Management objectives using ratio·analysis
16. 'Interfirm' comparison of companies
17. Types of reports in management information systems
18. Management accounting
19. Framework for a management accounting system
20. Budgeting principles
21. Budgetary control procedure
22. Weaknesses of budgetary control
23. Forecasting
24. Budgeting
25. Key questions for examining any activity or expense
26. Classification of overheads
27. Overhead allocation
28. Commonsense overhead allocations
29. Absorption costing versus direct costing
30. Flow of manufacturing costs in variable costing
31. Flow of manufacturing costs in absorption costing
32. Cost recording requirement
33. Cost control
34. Break-even analysis and graph
35. Cash management
36. Working capital
37. Working capital cycle
38. Action to improve cash flow cycle
39. Overtrading
40. Bankers/Lenders criteria
41. Insurance
42. Company acquisitions
43. Mergers

Foreword

SIR PETER PARKER, M.V.O.,
CHAIRMAN, BRITISH RAIL

There is no doubt in my mind that this book is necessary: it simplifies, it summarises, it insists on the obvious so often dangerously taken for granted, it hunts hard the blessed details. That is the point of the Checklist approach.

Any manager today needs to call on an armoury of skills. First, inevitably, technical competence. There must be a basis of knowledge, by training and experience, which produces the professional skill to combine through administration resources with markets to some profitable end — this is the essential and professional dimension and it is measurable.

Secondly, there is the dimension of entrepreneurial judgement, this is less measurable but crucial too. Here is the capacity for risk taking and risk making which makes all the difference between administration and business. Having looked hard at the selection of options, there must be a capacity still to leap, to land on the preferred option.

Thirdly, and increasingly important in our modern industrial society, is the call for social skills. The social realities are that a manager can only implement the preferred option if he can convince his social partners — his fellow managers and staff, that his sense of priorities makes common sense. And so it is that business management is nowadays in a context, almost a continuum, of consoltation and negotiation.

The value of any Checklist is not that it aims to teach necessarily, but aims to remind and to provide a controlled process for decision making. Furthermore it deploys information in such a way as to establish a logical approach to problem solving. This book seems to me to effectively link the essential skills of management. It must improve the entrepreneurial skill by more clearly evaluating the alternatives offered, and thus more clearly defining the risks. And this lays the foundation for more effective communication in the achievement of consent to action.

For my part this is the particular value of this Checklist: this book forces a full view of the responsibilities of the decision maker in their daunting variety. I suppose there are some people who can dismiss Checklists; all these things they do as a matter of course and logically. Others, more fallible, will draw some reassurance and indeed guidance and, more, a widening of vision. Far too often in our functional and departmental concentration, we lose sight of the size and shape of the wood as we study our own separate organisations trees. *The Businessman's Complete Checklist* reflects the range that is now necessary in the manager's armoury to deal with enterprise 'in the round'. Businessman? Superman?

Peter Parker
April 1978

List of Diagrams

1　Corporate Planning

1.1. BASIC PRINCIPLES OF COMPANY PLANNING

The purpose of company planning is to create the conditions today for the company to become aware of future market opportunities and to avoid dangers.

It is concerned with four questions:
Where does the company stand now?
What are its goals for the future?
How are its objectives to be reached?
What decisions must be taken now?

Effective planing stems from

Creative thinking
Use of a planning system
Sound knowledge of the company and its market
The choice of different options
Co-ordination

What do you need to know to plan ahead for the company?

Two main parts:
Producing a plan:
What is necessary
What is possible
How it can be done
Results of plan

Application of plan:
Management needed
Controls
Systems
Organization

1.2 PLANNING CONCEPT

Planning can be:
forward
future
strategic
corporate
long term

the motivation:

an increase on the return from effort
the more effective utilisation of resources

need answers to:

What is the corporate aim?
Why is it necessary to aim or set targets?
Where will the company be if the targets are not achieved?
Who will be assigned the task of defining the aims or objectives, then implementing them?
When should the anticipated plans materialise?
How will the plans be fulfilled and measured?

A planning system which has no built-in mechanism to ensure the conversion of short term plans and long term plans to a course of action is unlikely to achieve its purpose.

PLANNING — two main areas

the external environment
the internal environment

External environment
market penetration
competition
government legislation
financial availability

Internal environment
materials
production facilities and efficiency
labour relations
costs
cash flow

1.3 PLANNING — THE CORPORATE ENTITY

STRATEGIC

INTERNAL
Review company objectives, Assess achievements & strengths & weaknesses

EXTERNAL
Assess, political economic legislative competitive environment

Revise objectives: profitability market share return on capital personnel social

Evaluate action options

Define strategic plan

TACTICAL

SHORT TERM

LONG TERM

Company Structure
Style of management
Business sector
Location
Diversification

Resources
Human
Finance
Facilities
Divestment

Products
Materials
Research
Development
Marketing

1.4 CORPORATE GOALS

Percentage market share — by product and/or territory
Cost of sales force as percentage of turnover
Ratios e.g. return on sales, on capital on pre-tax profits
An absolute level of sales
Minimum acceptable figure for customer complaints
Number of customer enquiries
Maximum figure for productive hours lost
Labour productivity ratio increases
Reduction in late deliveries
Maximum number of employees
Acceptable level for employee "wastage" rate
Maximum permitted variance from budget
Cost reduction target
Date for major events
Increase in contribution to overheads
Reduction in debtors as percentage of turnover

A *goal* is a corporate divisional or departmental target, a *standard of performance* is something which is individually assigned to a named person.

The importance of personal standards is that they provide a tool for ensuring that plans are converted into tasks people can do — and are expected to do.

1.5 THE CORPORATE PLAN IN OUTLINE

A *corporate plan* involves the setting of *corporate objectives.*

Ground rules affect the attainment of these objectives through
attitude to employers and customers
nature of the organisation's business
attitude to risk taking
attitude towards changing the capital structure
willingness to acquire other companies
willingness to recruit new management
generally

Plans

development	operational
divestment	manufacturing
diversification	production
new business	capacity
expansion	requirements
research and	marketing
development	sales
	administration
	finance
	manpower
	managerial
	non managerial
	capital expenditure

Monitoring and control
performance summary
analysis of variances
action
revised plan

1.6 THE CORPORATE PLAN IN DETAIL

Introduction
Aim and strategic path
Scope of plan and subsidiary plans

Assumptions
Economic: price levels, inflation etc
Social: industrial relations, pollution etc
Governmental: legislation etc

Primary objectives
Increase return on capital and earnings per share

Secondary objectives
Area of business or trading
Market penetration
Customers loyalty
Labour relations

Strength and weaknesses
Raw material dependence
Product reputation
Delivery schedule reputation
Service availability
New product innovations
Management structure
Worker participation and labour relations
Plan capacity

Statement of expected results
Quantification of strategies and aims to coincide with primary and secondary objectives

Risk and sensitivity
Special hazards interacting on probable achievement of strategy

Strategies
Revision of present strategies e.g. new licencing agreements required to enable sales targets to be met

Operational improvements
Expansion or rationalisation — creating facilities both permanent assets and human resources

Organisation and Management
Revision of area of management and administration
Recruitment policies

Diversification
Change in procedure of product manufacture and/or sales distribution network

Finance
Ascertainment of capital to enable plans to be fulfilled

Contingency Plan

Criteria for effective planning
The plan should be concise yet long enough to give a clear understanding of what is intended

All well prepared plans have a purpose

There is always more than one course of action

The course of action chosen must be properly defined, and the reason for the choice understood

A plan must show that the purpose can be attained

Results expected from the course of action chosen must be specified

If the plan is to result in individual tasks it must allocate responsibilities

Timescale
Complete long range plans in first 6 months of each accounting year to cover either 3 or 5 years from start of next accounting year

The master plan should be rolled forward annually so that a 3 or 5 year plan is available

Complete budgets (or operating plans) for first year of plan during last quarter of preceding year

Every plan should have a timetable attached.

1.7 PLANNING REQUIREMENTS

Planning requirement most needed when:

Company with a large capital investment

Vulnerable to changes in:
Competition
Technologies
New product development

Low liquid resources
Long lead time for change to be implemented
Products mainly completing their profit life
Only moderately competent management at all levels.
Low all round competence
Manufacturing industry
Slow response to competitors' activities
Few products, one or two predominating
Product model changes
Diversification never attempted or attempted unsuccessfully
Highly administrative to production staff ratio
Difficult company environment
Future of the company uncertain
Production orientated
Low synergy
Flexible posture necessary for the company's long term survival

Risk reduction
Choose strategies with lower adverse effects if assumptions wrong.
Devise contingency plans
List hedging actions

1.8 THREE KEY AREAS OF PLANNING

Strategic Planning

Choosing company objectives
Planning the organisation
Setting personnel policies
Setting financial policies
Setting research policies
Choosing new product lines
Acquiring a new trade
Deciding on non-routine capital expenditures

Management Planning

Formulating budgets
Planning staff levels
Formulating personnel practices
Working capital planning
Formulating advertising programmes
Deciding on research projects
Choosing product improvements
Deciding on plan rearrangement
Deciding on routine capital expenditures
Formulating decision rules for operational control
Measuring, appraising, and improving management efficiency

Operational Planning

Controlling recruitment
Implementing personnel policies
Controlling credit extension
Controlling placement of advertisements
Scheduling production
Controlling inventory
Measuring, appraising, and improving workers' efficiency

1.9 DECISION MAKING PROCESS

Define the problem; locate the critical factor

Determine the conditions for its solution, the need to meet objectives and the balance between present and future.

Analyse the problem, find the facts necessary to a solution and capable of being obtained. Know where facts stop and assumptions begin

Develop alternative solutions, including 'do nothing'

Choose between solutions using as criteria for choice risk, economy of effort, timing, limitation of resources

Make the solution effective

1.10 SYSTEMATIC APPROACH TO PLANNING

Initial stimulus
   Are you aware of the problem?

Identification of the problems
   Time spent in identifying and interpreting the problems saves money and effort

Quantify the problem and set
   the dimensions
   the priorities
   the resources
   the time levels

Review the available resources
   Have you knowledge, manpower, finance?

Establish numerous solutions
   Consider advantages and disadvantages

Select appropriate solution
   Apart from facts, hunch plays its part through human qualities and experience

Residual problems
   Consider the problems which arise from implementing original solutions

Implement the solutions
   Establish guidelines and monitor progress

Review actions
   Revise procedures

Re-enter planning cycle

1.11 INTEGRATED COMPANY PLANNING

Analysing and appraising the situation

Setting objectives

Assembling possible market strategies

Choosing the most favourable strategy
in the traditional markets or
by diversification

Developing individual plans for sales,
product development, production, manpower,
acquisitions, organisation, finance

Checking the individual plans against the
financial plan for profitability and need for new
capital

Integrating the individual plans against the
financial plan for profitability and need for new
capital

Integrating the individual plans with each other
and adjusting as necessary

Working out action plans

Budgeting

Comparing plan with actual

Modifying the strategy as necessary

Working out new individual plans

1.12 KEYS TO GROWTH

Systematically seek out, find and reach for growth products and growth markets
Employ organised programmers to seek and promote new business opportunities

Be self critical about adequacy of the present operations thereby presenting superior competitive abilities

Top management should be composed of courageous, adventurous executives who are driven by an energetic zeal to lead

Establish formal systems of discovering opportunities and offsetting extreme risks through statements of company goals. Aim at creativity

Establish through the Chief Executive, an organisation environment of self-examina-ation and effervescent high adventure

Accept that even through the cautious practicing of corporate planning, there is still no guarantee of success; bad decisions may not be eliminated but without planning it is still possible for companies to be successful, but not many

Corporate planning will fail where:
The Chief Exective does not believe in it and senior management commitment does not exist

The Chief Executive allows no-one but himself to make decisions
Time cannot be found to write down plans or develop the strategy

Company planner is not reporting directly to Chief Executive

There is no desire for better results than have been achieved without planning

Hasty declarations of company objectives

Lack of appreciation of value of planning

The company is sinking so fast that, in any case, planning doesn't matter

Return on Capital Pyramid

1.14 BUSINESS RELOCATION

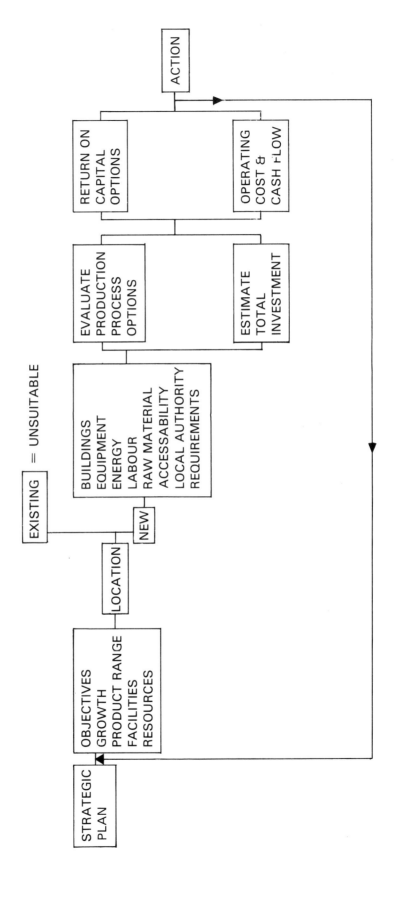

Business Relocation:

Government restrictions on development
Business growth
Shortage of labour
Technological change
Optimum size reached
Releases capital in present premises

Investigate:

Sales forecasts
Labour costs
Labour availability
Equipment/construction facilities
Sites
Materials
Utilities
Government regulations
Financing

Note any decision must bear in mind:

Profitability
Expansion at existing locations
Manufacturing own products
Continuing in present type of business
Flexibility of proposed facilities
Future changes of processes, etc.
Location: Consider transportation as proportion of total cost; the alternatives available, and over-dependence on local supplies

Industrial Concentration:

Present size firm
Remote and rural locations
Growth of business
Executive preference
Site availability
Labour availability

Advantages:

Proximity to market
Reduction of transport costs
Availability of Labour
Prestige of location
Contact with customers and competitors
Contact with Government departments (London)
Transport links
Educational facilities
Personal contacts with colleagues

Availability of specialist services, e.g. banking, insurance, maintenance services and stocks of products

Disadvantages:

Lack of space
Premises difficult and costly to acquire
High staff turnover — scarcity and expense of labour
Street and traffic congestion
Long journeys between home and workplace
Local competition
More militant labour force

When planning a move the following are necessary for success:

Proper co-ordination and control
Looking far enough ahead to the future
Not accepting status quo as basis
Business requirements — buildings, etc

Planning must include:

Sales forecasts
Product requirements
Make or buy analysis
Process layouts and flow process charts
Review of all production equipment and new equipment requirements
Re-examination of machine capacities
Materials handling and stores requirements
Detailed factory layouts — some of the factors to be taken into account are:
    The material flow pattern
    The site
    Routing of services
    The need for flexibility
    The production area
    Personnel movement
    Location of noisy dirty processes
Schedules of new and existing plant
Ordering and delivery dates of new equipment
Maintenance requirements for plant and buildings
Location of services requirements
Administrative organisation
Final plant layouts
Time schedules for the implementation of the above
Building specifications

Disposal of plant and equipment at old location

The financial analysis of project involves a complete financial analysis not only during the initial decision but also during the planning. This must include capital expenditure and profit and loss projections

Use decision trees, discounted cash flow and risk analysis techniques for choosing courses of action, but the final decision will be partially subjective

Financial control regarding capital expenditure sanctions, revisions of capital and operating budgets and actual expenditure is essential

The main areas for Capital Budget Expenditure are:

> Land
> Buildings
> Equipment
> Transfer and start up expenses

Note also:
Revenue from existing premises and possible Government financial aid

Personnel:
> Tell employees as soon as possible about the relocation
> Negotiate with employee representatives and trade unions
> Use manpower planning to establish staffing levels
> Arrange redundancy/termination arrangements

> When selecting staff to be transferred to a new location, consider:
> The cost advantages of transferring
> The manpower availability at the new location
> Availability of housing and other facilities for staff moved
> Reaction of population at the new location to influx of newcomers
> Desirable to take jobs and not people to a Development Area
> Desirable to take people not jobs to a New Town

Assistance:
> No change of residence — reimburse travelling costs (period of 1 year) allow for extra travelling time adjust salary

Change of residence:
> Expenses paid visits to new area (employees and dependents)
> Liaison with local house agents
> Reimbursement of legal and professional fees
> Removal expenses paid
> Expenses paid house-hunting visits
> Disturbance allowance
> Interest free loans
> Travelling costs from temporary accommodation
> Recruitment of new staff

> > Organise facilities
> > Set up interview stages

The Move:
> A sufficiently senior member of management must be appointed
> The location must be independent in terms of administration and self-government

Problems experienced:

> Design and construction deficiencies
> Delays in the provision of service facilities by the local town administration
> Numerous minor problems, e.g. lights, drainage, etc.
> Equipment necessary after the move
> Insufficient preparation of maintenance procedures
> The effectiveness and efficiency of the processing lines did not rise as fast as anticipated

General Points:

The majority of business can stand the disruptive effects of relocation. It may take quite some time for these to disappear and it will be the smaller firm that may not be able to stand these disruptions

In the main, there are few substantial costs savings to be made as a result of relocation

1.15 MANAGEMENT DO'S AND DON'TS

Don't sell what you haven't got

Don't take on more business than you can cope with

Don't take on work against another person's design without safeguards as to workability, design changes, price and delivery

Don't sell to a specification you haven't achieved

Don't make 'specials' for which there is no general demand unless it is your business

Do ensure that product costs are realistic and reliable

Do introduce stable management policies

Do cut out loss making parts of the business and improve operations with low returns on capital employed

Do assume that there might be a better way of doing anything until the contrary is proved

Do remember that it is usually a relatively small amount of effort which produces most of the return

Do accept that often knowledge of what is being done is not as perfect as managers believe

Do recognise that the future is more important than the present

See Also

2 Management

Business is concerned with transactions in the market place and with supplying a service or buying, making and selling.

Business houses are like other systems and are capable of being analysed and synthesized.

To understand a business one must know

What is its overall purpose
How it is to be achieved
How to determine the most effective organisation of resources; people, money, raw materials
How the change its corporate strategy to meet changing market place needs

To run a business efficiently means to run it profitably with appropriate economic return on total capital invested: people, money and raw material

Long term and short term profits must be weighed against each other

There can be many individual businesses within a company

Businesses within a company require to be appraised regularly covering the following problem areas:

Products and the customers' appraisal of them
Capability of the sales organisation
Production facilities and their technological status and economic viability
Development of the market with respect to the market size, the technical demands on the product, the structure of the customers, the sales channels and the competition
Capability of the business or company for adapting its product and its selling methods to the future demands of the market

Market planning and financial planning occupy a central position:

Centralised

v

Decentralised

Centralised

Advantages:

Strong authority at the top where overall decisions are made because it is the meeting point of all information

Easy recruitment of middle managers usually promoted from the ranks

Disadvantages:

The whole firm depends on one man to grasp everything, and whose replacement becomes very difficult. Who tends to become authoritative, refusing dialogue and delegation of authority

The department managers are not able to make sophisticated decisions and to overcome their specialisation; neither are middle managers, whose promotion is difficult due to their lack of preparation in supervising activities

Contacts between technical and marketing functions are made at the top and impede good comprehension of numerous techniques and diversified markets

The whole system depends on command or negotiations. It prevents initiative and flexibility

Decentralised

Advantages:

It frees top management from having to make short-term decisions

It helps to fix accountability, spreads out responsibility, and motivates managers who become responsible for their performance and can evaluate it

It is very flexible, permits handling diversified techniques and markets, for it brings the decision-making closer to the scene of action
It fosters initiative

Disadvantages:

It requires capable managers

The decentralised unit may become so independent that it may actually begin to work against the interests of the company as a whole

The manager may maximise short-term gains at the expense of long-term goals.
He may show outstanding results for a time by not replacing tangible assets when he should, by overloading customers, or cutting down research

Decentralisation increases administrative expense, since many of the staff functions at headquarters have to be duplicated in the divisions if the division manager is to do the job properly

Top management must be strong for it is its responsibility to avoid these risks and control consistency between decentralised unit operations and corporate objectives

What kind of a structure does a business need to perform its job effectively?

What activities are necessary to achieve the purpose of the business?
What decisions will have to be made?
What relationships are necessary between the people forming the structure?

The attitude of the Chief Executive is crucial, one must:

help to set demanding corporate goals
reshape the organisation to fulfil the goals required;
encourage an awareness of change in all aspects of company environment
motivate cooperation, communication, collaboration and interdependence in all managerial roles
encourage the development of applicable corporate strategies
monitor the effectiveness of these strategies
develop suitable managerial incentives

Improvement of performance by providing means with which each manager can monitor and help improve his or her standard

Management by objectives requires certain basic steps on the part of management. Any MBO system must include:

reviewing critically and restating the company's strategic and tactical plans

clarifying with each manager his key results and performance standards and gaining his contribution and commitment to these — the relationship between each manager must be fully understood so that teamwork is facilitated

establishing rigorous procedures for control and self-control of progress — this will always include performance and potential review

establishing imaginative management development programmes, including training plans, selection, salary and succession plans

providing conditions in which these results can be achieved, this means a supportive climate of opinion, effective organisation structure and sound management control information

Problems encountered when applying MBO

distrust by employees
resentment by management
problems of management commitment to written assessment
need for management to set valid objectives
lack of data
need for top management backing

Implementation of Management by Objectives

Introduction to senior management — total involvement and acceptance required
Set Management Guides
a) results analysis
area under consideration
standard expected
standard achieved
b) job description
main purpose
position in organisation
size of job
limits of authority

Agree with managers
Set timescale for plan
Review performance

Measure of success

ratio of internal placements to external appointments
management standards rise with more professional approach
better organisation structures
more accountability within the structure
more emphasis on training for specfic performance improvement

Definition: **A Manager**

Needs no supervision

Is responsible for the functioning of his unit all the time, whether he is there or not

Writes, transmits and applies the rules for his unit

Does not allow an employee to occupy a post or undertake a task for which he is not trained

Delegates but does not abdicate

Knows his reputation is less important than that of the group

Ensures someone is responsible for every task at every moment

Looks at his unit through the customers eyes

Ensures his personnel concentrate on service even when they are very busy

Sets up a strong team to maintain standards of quality and service in his unit. The strength of his team determines his promotion prospects

Is interested in his staff members, and provides them with:

technical training
commercial motivation
the practice of responsibility

Must be investigative, adaptable, available

The Manager's role:

Set objectives and goals for each work area and to plan how to reach those goals

Organise work. To analyse, divide and allocate work to groups and individuals

Motivate and communicate. To create a team to provide incentives of the right kind and the information which people need

Measure results. To check against plans see that each man knows what he is doing and where he fits in

Develop people — or to manage them in a way which enables them to develop themselves

Fundamental to the success for business is managing of managers. Management is the one function which operates only on people and in a wide variety of circumstances. Every manager, by and large, has under him people who manage other people.

The way in which managers are managed determines the level of performance of the management effort.

From the performance of the management effort stems the performance of the business or enterprise

A manager in managing subordinates must:

Ensure that the vision, wills and efforts of his subordinates are directed to the goals of the business, i.e. total commitment to laid-down objectives

Structure his subordinates jobs so that they are able to perform effectively, i.e. analyse, divide and allocate work to groups and individuals

Create the right spirit in which the team element can develop; to motivate and communicate and measure achievements

Take steps to develop his subordinates to provide tomorrows higher levels; help them to develop themselves

A manager develops through:

Sincere objective appraisal of performance

Financial rewards directly related to performance

Job satisfaction

A promotion system based on performance

Each job structured in such a way that the definition and limits are laid down e.g. division of work, authority and responsibility, discipline, unity of direction, stability, conditions and iniative are all pre-requisites to the measurement of performance

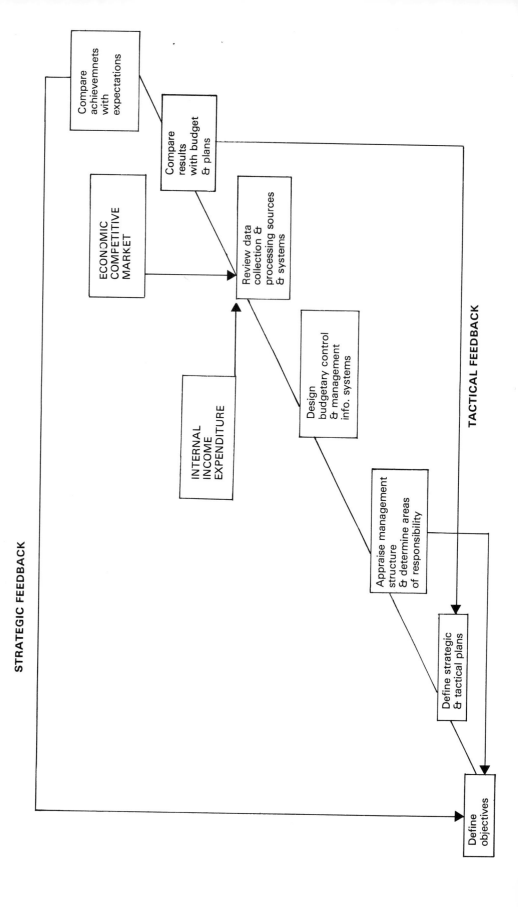

2.7 MANAGEMENT INFORMATION SYSTEMS

STRATEGIC FEEDBACK

TACTICAL FEEDBACK

Compare achievemnets with expectations

Compare results with budget & plans

ECONOMIC COMPETITIVE MARKET

Review data collection & processing sources & systems

INTERNAL INCOME EXPENDITURE

Design budgetary control & management info. systems

Appraise management structure & determine areas of responsibility

Define strategic & tactical plans

Define objectives

DATA CATCHMENT	DATA CONVERSION	DATA OUTPUT
A. ENVIRONMENTAL Social Political Economic		PROFIT AND LOSS STATEMENTS Company Division Unit Department
B. COMPETITIVE Market Share Past Performance Present Activity Strategic Plans		NET ASSET STATEMENTS Company Division
C. ACCOUNTING Financial Accounting Management Accounting		CASH MOVEMENT MANAGEMENT RATIOS FORECASTS — SHORT TERM

Is information presented in such a way that it assists in decision-making?

Does information indicate each responsible individual's achievements and level of required performance? Are responsibilities clearly defined?

Does the information presented to him enable the individual manager to make plans and set standards?

Do reports present both results and — insofar as possible — the reasons behind these results?

Are past and present levels of performance emphasized in reports?

Is the reporting structure flexible?

Are established goals and other standards stressed as benchmarks in reports?

Is information about the future given in reports?

Is information of a non-financial nature reported where it has relevance to financial outcomes?

Is information on external conditions (as they might bear on a particular organization's operations) given in reports?

Is each report oriented towards its recipient, considering both his level and function?

Do reports give as much information as possible in quantitative terms?

Are reports suitably succinct? Is exception reporting encouraged?

Are recipients of reports urged to consider fully their content and to discuss this with colleagues and staff?

Is an appropriate and known degree of accuracy secured in reported information?

Does management realize that the study of management information and reporting systems is not necessarily concerned with computers?

Is it understood that more data in reports does not in itself mean more information for management?

Does management know that information needs cannot all be predetermined by systems studies?

Is it appreciated that for information to be instantly available does not necessarily increase its value or usefulness? And that frequent reporting does not necessarily mean that information is thereby more useful? Half accurate information on time is better than totally correct information too late.

Is management by exception practised in designing and compiling reports?

Are reports understood?

Is unnecessary detail eliminated from reports?

Do reports call the attention of higher levels of management to those situations that cannot be controlled at lower levels?

Is each report that is produced really necessary?

Can reports be condensed, or combined one with another?

Can the frequency of issue of reports be altered?

Is an interest in the reporting system maintained at all levels of management?

Can significant figures be produced and communicated between normal reporting dates?

Are regular review meetings held to consider reports, results, and the adequacy of reporting systems?

Are attempts made to explain variations from plan in an upwards direction in the organization before criticism proceeds downwards to the source of variation?

Are the duties and responsibilities of all those concerned with producing reports clearly defined?

Is the chart of accounts compatible with the requirements of the reporting system? Does either take precedence?

Are controllable expenses segregated from those that are non-controllable?

Are results reported in the same manner in which managers plan and think about their operations?

Are reports presented in an easy-to-read format?

Is appropriate use made of ratios and percentages?

Are figures in reports rounded whenever possible?

Is follow-up properly planned?

Can the reader grasp easily the developments from the reports, act on these or ensure other action

2.9 NEW PROBLEMS FACING MANAGEMENT

New and flexible approaches to management thinking are required to meet a new social conscience within a framework of existing social and economic problems

How much control should workers have?

What status should they have based on their social contribution?

What is the social value of the individual?

What are reasonable or good working conditions?

How much involvement should unions be offered?

Should worker directors be appointed?

Should share/profit schemes be offered?

How does inflation affect the Unions?

Cash flow problems and erosion of the capital base with ever increasing cost spiral for raw material

Increasing government participation requirements

Strength or vulnerability of the pound for exports

Stop-go policy with regard to credit from the Exchequer

Competition from Abroad

Hankering after decentralization needs strong central policies

2.10 DECISION MAKING

What kind of a structure does a business need to perform its job effectively?

What activities are necessary to achieve the purpose of the business?

What decisions will have to be made?

What relationships are necessary between the people forming the structure?

Decision making process:

Define the problem

Locate the critical factor

Determine the conditions for its solution, the need to meet objectives and the balance between present and future

Analyse the problem

Find the facts necessary to a solution and capable of being obtained

Know where facts stop and assumptions begin

Develop alternative solutions; including 'do nothing'

Choose between solutions using as criteria for choice, risk, economy of effort, timing limitation of resources

Make the solution effective

2.11 RESPONSIBILITY ACCOUNTING

Are individuals' responsibilities clearly defined?

Is the assigned authority in line with delegated responsibility in all cases?

Is delegation properly carried out?

Is the organization chart current, adequately detailed, and available to all staff?

Could any organizational grouping be reorganized to reduce costs or improve effectiveness?

Are objectives — both corporate and departmental — established and communicated?

Are key assignments rotated? Should they be; and, if so, can they be?

Is management succession planned?

Are responsibilities divided in such a way as to permit a budgetary measurement of individual effectiveness?

Are all responsible individuals called upon to explain variances in their areas? Are follow-up actions checked?

Is every necessary function unambiguously assigned to a responsibility centre?

Are responsibilities specific and understood?

Is there any overlapping of responsibilities?

Does each individual within the organization have one — and only one — boss?

Does an adequate coding system exist so that all cost items can readily be recorded in their proper account?

Does the chart of accounts accurately represent the organisational structure as it is rather than as it perhaps should be? Does the management information system reflect the structure?

Are all items of expense recorded in accordance with the lowest level or area of operations to which they can be directly related?

Are all needless allocations and apportionments avoided?

2.11 RESPONSIBILITY ACCOUNTING
(cont)

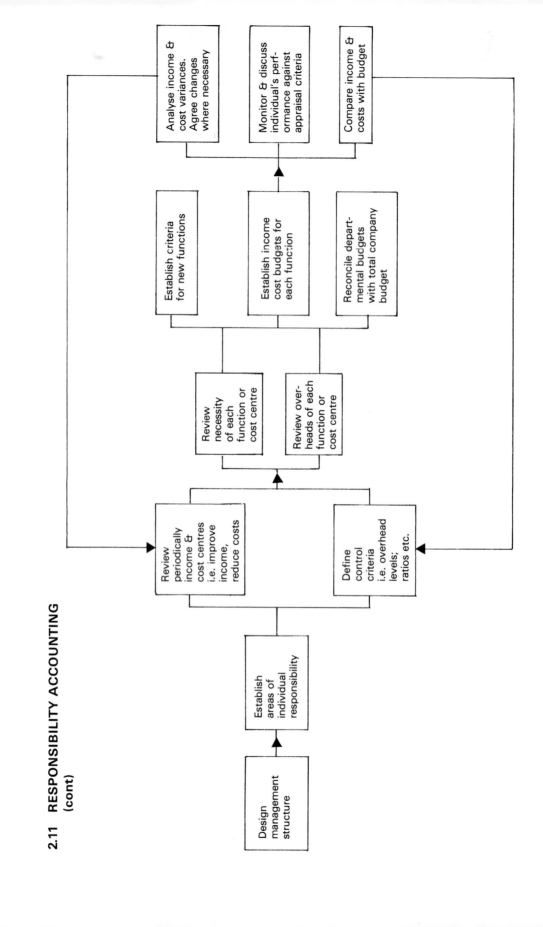

Are all changes in responsibilities made with a clear understanding of their impact on the part of all concerned?

Are all cases of promotion, salary increases, and disciplinary action approved by the immediate superior of the individual?

Do all disputes over questions relating to authority and responsibility receive prompt and careful consideration?

Are accurate standards set for each measurable and controllable cost element?

Are all costs clearly split into their controllable and uncontrollable categories (bearing in mind the level of authority and the time span)?

Is cost consciousness encouraged throughout the organization?

Do cost controls correspond with areas of organisational responsibililty?

Is the performance of each responsible individual regularly measured, monitored and reported?

Are the plans/standards used in performance measurement adequate and sufficiently accurate?

Discussion and arrangement of terms of transaction or agreement:

Levels:
person to person
group to group
organisation to organisation
international negotiations

Selection of committee:
Is it representative?
Has it status and authority for credibility?
Do not include senior management.
Include members who will administer agreement.
Include younger members to gain experience.

Information useful to committee:
Age, length service etc.
Personal connection and concerns.
General details (hobbies etc.)
Reasons why on committee.

General:
Use visual aids, e.g. graphs etc.
Direct attention towards quantifiable numbers
Preparation requires discipline
Humour is a valuable aid and its use can be encouraged.
Allocate issues to members according to individual credibility,
Allocate responsibility for taking notes during meeting.
Write agenda

Impasse:
Have all possible information, positions, compromises, evaluations and emotions been extracted from the discussion?
What are the possibilities of reaching tentative agreement on the issue?
Are there other issues which should be resolved before reaching tentative agreement on this one?
What are the implications of being the party that recommends passing it for the present?
Will further discussion only serve to further harden existing positions and threaten agreement on other issues.

Specific Uses:

> Current planning
> Long-term planning
> Testing potential
> Research & Development
> Capital investment
> Cash flow
> Financing (short and long-term)
> Manpower
> Distribution
> Production
> Raw materials
> Selling

Problems in Forecasting:

> Unrecognisable patterns
> Non-comparable situations
> New factors
> Slow changes
> Cycles: econometric
>   seasonal

To help overcome these problems select the approach noting:

> What will the forecast be used for?
> What risks are there in the forecast?
> What is the forecast time scale?
> What period of historical data is available?
> What information is there available on similar activities?
> What accuracy is required?
> What time is available to prepare?
> What revisions will be possible?

Approach to forecasting:
> Statistical Analysis
> Subjective Judgement

Design Shortcomings:

> Bad location and design of service areas
> Inflexible design
> Physical conditions (e.g. noise, light etc.)
> Faults (e.g. slippery floors etc.)
> Maintenance (e.g. high cost and difficulty in cleaning)
> Large proportion of unusable space (e.g. stairs, corridors etc.)

To avoid these faults:

> set up small project team (possible varying composition during project)
> give team a closely involved chairman

Budgets must:

specify require-ments	state flexibility
	give cost analysis
state location	discuss finance

Types of building contract:
> tendering
> negotiation
> 'Package'

Technical problems:

noise	site composition
smell	size
dust	shape
daylight	drainage

Office environment:

illumination level	noise levels
daylight	space
colour	communications
design	telephone, mail
temperature	flexibility
draughts	office machinery
humidity	filing
rate of change of air	general storage

Note: For every new building a booklet should be produced for all staff, showing the layout, services

Applications

to present facts, concepts and information in a structured and effective form

to create positive attitudes, or correct negative one, towards, an industry, product, service, concept

to create new opportunities to reach specific individuals or groups

to gain attention (at exhibition, trade shows etc)

to motivate their audiences, towards a positive decision

Situations of Use — direct promotion of a product or service via:

invited customer gatherings

face to face presentations on desk top projectors to individual customers

planned non-theatrical library distribution

point of sale promotions in retail outlets

public relations activities, particularly for general marketing development purposes

internal information e.g. induction

new product launches

internal sales training

retailer/dealer sales training and information servicing training, and as a form of service manual particularly for dealers

product information programmes (up-dating information)

exhibitions and trade shows

direct promotion to the specific market sectors

Briefing of Audio Visual Team

role in the total marketing communications context

audience attitudes to be created

who precisely are the groups and individuals that need to be reached?

what are their existing attitudes to and preknowledge of the programme subject?

which audio-visual distribution media is most suitable?

what communication opportunities can be created in which the audio-visual message can be presented to the intended audiences

in what environment(s) will the audience(s) receive the message? office, exhibition, hotel etc?

what support is required from other media? — brochures, handbooks

the cost parameters which the production and distribution objectives entail

Remember that an audio-visual aid helps a poor speaker

it is a 'normal' and expected medium to use at a presentation

retention is aided by the production of leaflets, brochures etc., for people to take away

use the full range of effects available with each audio-visual medium because the audience expects professionalism

a professional, practical presentation is always needed with audio-visual aids for speaking

the audio-visual aid can never do the whole job — needs the help of the presenter to set the scene

2.16 TYPES OF AUDIO VISUAL AID MEDIA

16mm film:

    flexible
    range of effects
    expensive
    long production time
    difficult to change or update
    needs external production
    widely used
    good quality large picture
    poor daylight viewing
    distribution outlets available

Slide with Audio Tape:

    easy to incorporate amendments
    multi image/screen effects
    simple to have different versions of one
    programme
    can be produced in house
    slides easy to obtain
    good impact
    adaptable for small/large gatherings

Video:

    easy to use
    'normal' medium view
    heavy, non mobile equipment
    incompatability between makes
    limited audience size
    quick to produce
    no good for fine detail
    primarily "studio" based
    immediate replay

Overheard projector slides:

    cheap
    poor quality
    unsuitable large audience

Flip Charts

    very cheap
    difficult to read
    easily damaged

2.17 INDUSTRIAL MANAGEMENT PROBLEMS

Achieving partnership between Government and business in public service while preserving competitive outlook — retention of virtues of both systems

Becoming trusted by Government as public servants accountable to them — given delegated responsibility and authority and bringing about withdrawal of Governments from detailed restraints and interference with industry

Obtaining willing acceptance of planned economy and mixed economy by business and by Government

Development, management and direction of foreign affiliates, with appropriate degrees of private or public national participation in ownership and/or management

Age and succession. Retiring age and longevity

Adjusting industry to democratic tendencies — questions of centralisation and decentralisation

Size and scale

Efficiency and productivity and of permitted degrees of co-operation

Finance — take-overs, mergers, retained profits

Engineering — of development and applied science, as contrasted with pure science, physics and chemistry

Paternalism, associated with growth and remoteness, and problems of human sensitivity sufficient to pioneer and anticipate

Inevitability of technology and the need to harness it

Financial resources in ever expanding economies, and of foreign currency needs

Commercial and investment policies

Redundancies and technical progress

Weighing up world-wide excessive demand against pressures for shorter hours and less work

Advertising and selling, including restraints to damp down inflationary spending

Personal responsibilites of community leadership for industrial leaders — local or national

Education and training right up to senior management, with emphasis on recruitment, training and promotion of potential leaders

Early selection of future leaders

Acquiring mentality to welcome unsuspected future changes as well as past

Communications upwards and downwards inwards and outwards

Personality, of touch

Distribution — poverty amid plenty

Spreading the best management technique round the world

How to make the manager with a specialist skill into a leader able to take quick decisions over a wider front

How to prevent large businesses becoming too departmental and too full of specialists

3 Marketing and Selling

3.1 FORMULATION OF MARKETING PLAN

Research work needed

General:

How does marketing research expenditure compare with competitors?

What marketing research has been accomplished in home and export markets?

How effective was it?

Has the firm efficient information sources?

What data is there available?

What methods of marketing research have been found to be effective?

What experimentation is taking place?

Are independent agencies preferred to firms own research?

How can product intelligence be obtained?

Market:

total size of market
rate of change of size
factors affecting changes
number of competitors
competitors' market share
competitors' change in market share
competitors' sales organisation structure
ruling current market prices
forecasts of market conditions
seasonal/cyclical market fluctuations
market potential (new and existing)
user characteristics/attitudes/opinions
potential customers — kind, number and location
product uses
customers' product selection criteria (e.g. performance size, shape, service
sources of customer dissatisfaction
competitive position of company products
distribution methods

3.2 INFORMATION REQUIRED FOR MARKETING PLAN

Economic:

industry cycles	deliveries
profits	unemployment
share prices	production
gross national product	gross domestic product
order/sales cycle	profit cycle & trends
investment cycle	trends of activity (growth/decline)

Political:

Price Commission or similar body
regional development
monopolies
wage restraint

Social and Environmental Legislation:

pollution	working
lighting	heating
ventilation	noise
legislation	scarce resources

pressure for recycling of natural resources

Competitors' Activities:

competition's strengths and weaknesses in pricing policy

attitude to fixed price contracts and escalation

pricing policies — flexible prices reigning

servicing policy

type of distribution/selling cover

promotion activity/mail shots/product catalogues/operators and services manuals

policy to debtors/creditors leasing

patents restricting market

substitute product evaluation

market outlet — degree sophistication

level service required

potential purchasing power total market

strength/weaknesses product within market

growth/decline of market

Sampling:

Cheaper and quicker than a 100 per cent survey.

A higher quality survey because of a smaller sample size.

Sample size depends on degree of precision, but allow for non-response.

Accuracy and power of the forecast required

Use past to estimate the future but guage importance

Terms of Reference:

information required
timescale
budget
sources available
scope of survey
decisions to be made from survey

Conducting the Survey

Questionnaire design:

unstructured — uses only interview guide
impossible to analyse
useful for formulating and checking ideas
can omit significant questions
and encourage irrelevances
semi-structured — standard questions cope
with most responses

ease of tabulation/analysis
ease of recording
questionnaire covers all points required
needs to be designed well
structured questionnaire
only for very simple information

Note: design questionnaire with:

space for easy recording answers
stimulating and orientating early questions
important questions early on

Method of Contact

Requirements of method chosen:

collect information speedily
produce information cheaply
cope with large volumes of information
generate quantitive information
produce new ideas
ask complex questions
probe in depth
give due weight to expert informants
protect against bias
check validity of the answers
explain divergence of opinions
ensure anonymity/confidentiality of
individual opinions

Personal interview:

expensive
slow (1 hour per person)
answers can be checked
probing/follow up questions

Telephone interview:

speed
lower cost
small volumes of information
no complex questions
avoid being nuisance
difficult to check answers
difficult to establish rapport
relieves salesmen of routine tasks

Postal questionnaire:

low cost
low unpredictable response rate (5 to 10 per cent)
follow-up mailings
can provide blanket coverage
no interview control
sensitive information will not be given
only a few questions to be asked

Group Discussions:

need six to ten people

3.4 MARKETING PLAN RESOURCE ALLOCATION

A Marketing orientated company places customers and their needs at centre of business

Marketing:

> fits a business to its customers' needs
> seeks to achieve more effective selling by looking ahead
> optimum profit from minimum cost
> aims to give direction and purpose to management

Resource allocations depend on:

> today's and tomorrow's winners
> productive specialities
> development products
> failures and their corrections
> repair jobs
> unnecessary specialities
> unjustified specialities
> investments in managerial ego

Allocation of key resources should be mainly to those products which will show worthwhile results

Today's winners are at or close to their peak and any excessive allocation of resources to them should be cut back

Results are obtained by exploiting opportunities not by solving problems alone

3.5 MARKETING DEPARTMENT ORGANISATION

From these produce systematic list of tasks for next 12 months in marketing department

What is required to know and be able to do tasks?

Should use be made of:

> External courses
> 'Tailored' courses (external)
> Internal courses
> Instruction and guided self development

Organisation

3 Key areas:
> Sales
> Product development
> New products

Training — identifying needs:

Marketing plan
> Department objectives
> Job descriptions

Personnel:

Consider the following:
> Basic training
> Job history
> Qualifications required
> Working relations required
> Functional relations required

3.5 MARKETING DEPARTMENT ORGANISATION (cont'd)

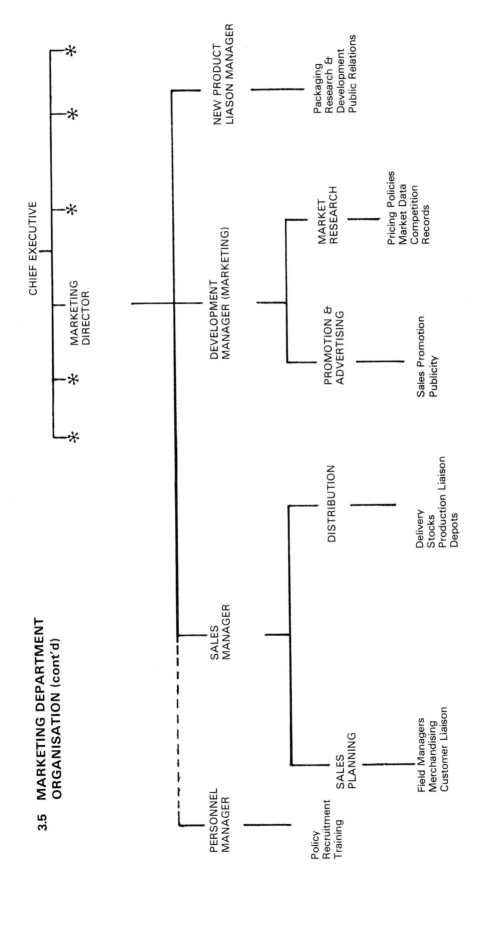

New products:

What market share can we expect if we continue on our present course?

How will customers requirements and habits change?

What new markets are suitable?

What will be their sales potential?

When will this potential be reached?

What will need to be done — development; production; sales?

What resources will be needed e.g. manpower?

Will financial resources be sufficient?

Will specialists be needed?

What will profit margin be?

Can we obtain an adequate market share?

How fast will the market grow?

How is the demand divided — Government/industrial/military/private?

What future market share can we expect if the products are modernised?

How will sales increase if we extend our product range?

Can our sales effort be intensified and what effect will this have?

Market changes:

How will competitors' demands affect product?

How will composition of customers change?

What will happen to price levels?

What government action may happen?

How will sales channels alter?

Are there any cyclical changes within the industry?

How strong is the product range of company X?

Are competitors likely to become more effective in the near future?

Are the markets for the products of company X growing or declining? How and why?

Will company X still be successful for the foreseeable future?

Stages in product acquisition:

exploration
screening
investigation
proposition
negotiation
integration

Key pitfalls:

Not placing responsibility at a sufficiently high level

Failing to establish a real unanimity of opinion as to what the acquisition objectives should be

Setting unrealistic criteria for to-day's competitive sellers' market

Searching only among companies for sale

Failing to recognise the time required for a successful acquisition programme

Failing to focus the search correctly

Failing to investigate prior to actual negotiations

Failing to assess correctly a seller's motives

Overlooking opportunities by using mechanical screening procedures

Failure to obtain qualified outside assistance when needed

Too much analysis and too little action; or vice-versa

Success criteria:

To establish clearly defined growth objectives

Sound internal organisation to establish acquisition criteria

Business strategy is expressed in products. Product programmes are the foundation of forward company planning

The new product programme is a top management responsibility

The new product function should be organised as a top executive staff function, headed by person who can work effectively at top management level

Organisation and control should be established in conformance with the stages of new product evolution:

exploration

↓

screening

↓

business analysis

↓

development

↓

testing

↓

commercialisation

Co-ordinated new product effort is best achieved through interdepartmental product teams, representing all functional areas of the business, tailored to fit the characteristics of each product

A definite programme, carefully planned and closely managed, significantly improves new product results

New idea creation can be directed and controlled to achieve improved pertinence and quality of product ideas

New product selection is accomplished by a continuing series of evaluations in all stages. No single screening is adequate

Selection standards for products to be developed should be upgraded persistently to achieve an ever-increasing yield from available manpower and resources

Product planning requires adequate specifications and a programme for each product prior to laboratory development

Market requirements and opportunities are the primary consideration in product planning

Company acquisition should be integrated with internal development to achieve a balanced new product programme.

3.9 NEW PRODUCT PLANNING STAGES

Screening:

> expand idea into a full product concept
> collect facts and opinions
> appraise idea for potential value
> test opinion
> produce written report

Business analysis:

> appoint production team for further study of idea
> determine feasibility of large scale production
> develop specifications and establish a definite programme for the product
> do preliminary market research
> set up timetable for product launch

Development:

> establish development projects for each product
> build product to designated or revised specifications
> complete laboratory evaluation and release for testing
> continue market research

Testing:

> plan commercial experiments necessary to test and verify earlier judgments of the product
> conduct in-use, production, and market testing
> make final product decision, freeze design

Commercialisation:

> complete final plans for production and marketing
> initiate co-ordinated production and selling programmes
> check results — make necessary improvements in product, manufacturing, or sales
> monitor design faults

3.10 DIRECT MAIL, ADVERTISING AGENCIES

Direct Mail

Mail sent to specific addresses for advertising prepared the way for the sales force and can act in these ways:

> advertising — influencing attitudes
> sales promotion — obtaining leads
> direct selling — obtaining sales

Advantages:

> selectivity
> personal approach
> nearly always looked at
> variety of formats
> flexibility
> reply paid response cards

> *Note:* bulk rebate system from the Post Office

Assessment of success:

> cost per reply
> number read by customers (from representatives' sales reports)

Advertising agencies

Because techniques are becoming increasingly complex and elaborate, the use of an agency is compelled to maintain quality

Research work should be separate from advertising agency:

> agencies do not generally have comprehensive research department
> possible bias within agency between creative and research sides

3.11 ADVERTISING CHECK LIST ON USE

Types of media:

> newspapers
> trade papers
> television
> radio
> cinema
> subscription journals
> business supplements
> posters
> placards
> direct mail
> exhibitions
> educational campaigns
> export journals
> institute publications
> other publications

Reason for use:

> changes opinions and attitudes — level of change depends on frequency and quality

market share depends on opinions of product

> significantly improves level of sales closings (especially where no regular customer contact)
> reduces costs of selling — if adequate frequency
> advertising in well advertised market increases cost of selling

Allocation of funds:

> existing production capacity
> saturation point where resources become limited or expensive
> rate of market response to extra sales and marketing effort
> future market growth potential
> use contribution figures after direct costs instead of sales figures
> use true gross profit to net profit monetary values instead of % figures (relieves the considerably confusion created thereby)
> cost product groups down to net profit contribution (show marketing support costs in each group)

Media strategy:

> Is the market horizontal (everybody) or vertical (selective)?

> Where the primary objective of a press campaign is to enhance the reputation of the advertiser, large spaces in horizontal media are most likely to succeed.

> When the primary objective is enquiries, small spaces in vertical media are usually more appropriate, particularly where a reader reply service is operated by the publisher

> Where the application of the product has distinct operational benefits, case-histories are often most effective

> Where advantages are in the price/delivery/quality areas, a generalised customer-benefit approach is appropriate

Measuring effectiveness:

> Aim
> to make advertising work harder and more effectively
> to use professional and creative people
> Do not
> assume you know your present and potential customers
> use a publication or programme just because you like it
> approach advertising with preconceived ideas
> produce advertising that just pleases your boss
> forget it is the effects of advertising that are most important — these must be measured

Techniques:

- press releases
- handouts
- receptions and conferences
- open days
- facility and informal visits
- shareholders' meetings
- prestige films
- corporate status adveritising
- radio and TV participation in programmes
- sponsorship

Types of press release:

- case histories
- unusual product uses
- company magazines/brochures
- contract/order announcements
- sales milestones
- continuity of supply
- quality control
- after-sales service
- factory/plant development
- research activities
- policy changes
- marketing changes
- special promotions
- new staff appointments
- first/large/unusual export order
- record output
- participation in overseas trade exhibitions

Factors for new/modified product announcements:

- description
- cost
- availability
- applications
- prospective purchasers
- competitors' product comparison
- sales offices addresses
- dealer details
- promotions available
- research details
- outline other new products
- photographs

Customer loyalty:

- how many suppliers to customer?
- how long have they been?
- rate of change of suppliers?
- rate of change of business between suppliers?
- how easy is it to change?

Suppliers' image:

Product attributes	*Suppliers' attributes*
quality	reliable delivery
performance	quick delivery
reliability	technical service
appearance	and advice
price	attention to complaints
ease of maintenance	order handling
full range	credit terms
	discounts
	commercial services

Competition activity:

- increasing/decreasing
- product comparison
- pricing
- availability

Market share ratios:

- cost per £x sales
- cost per customer serviced
- cost per sales transaction
- cost per £x gross contribution
- average selling cost per unit
- selling prices
- discount structures
- relative sales mixes
- gross/net contribution per representative
- gross/net contribution per sales area
- gross/net contribution per distribution area
- gross/net contribution per order
- administration costs (sales)

3.14 SALES FORCE STANDARDS OF PERFORMANCE

Is ratio of contracts/orders received to quotations submitted;

> increasing?
> static?
> decreasing?

Do we qualify needs and degree of interest of enquirer?

Do we establish:

> whether quotation is for future reference?
> whether purchase depends upon other negotiations?
> a firm intent to purchase?
> when completion/delivery is required?
> competitive involvement?
> maximum price?
> clear understanding of requirements?
> probability of successful negotiations?
> a provisional estimate prior to full quote?

Define size and type of quotation which should not require executive involvement

Institute a standard follow-up procedure — by correspondence/telephone

Submit reports of progress towards completion of negotiations

Quotations:

> Does the layout and general appearance of our quotations compare favourably with that of our competitors?
> For certain low-priced quotations, consider image, may appear too expensive to the customer?
> Are any people singularly successful in converting quotations into firm orders —
> if so, analyse methods used
> in the event of a contract or order being lost, obtain the true reason for failure
> indicate Conditions of Sale on every written quotation
> Endeavour to make 'on site' quotations for low-cost work and seek additional work at same time

3.15 CALL REPORTS

Completion of reports:

Do not waste management time by writing superfluous and unusable information, but do transmit essential information for prompt action

Reports from salesmen can show:

> value of sales
> number of sales
> category of sale
> sales target per period
> attainment towards target
> number of calls made
> number of new prospects found
> reason for no sale
> length of each interview
> quality of prospect
> number and date of return calls
> new accounts opened
> name and address of all calls
> complaints
> enquiries
> request for quotations
> progress on enquiries/quotations
> competitive activity

Analysis of Reports:

Use reports and records of salesmen to reveal average
> call rate
> length of interview
> percentage of travelling time
> value of orders
> number of enquiries passed from head office
> conversion ratio of orders to enquiries

Are sales territory boundaries clearly defined
Are maps of sales territories issued to salesmen
Calculate the 'new business' potential in possible expanding areas
Are sales territories in line with possible increase of salesmen

Why were you selling to him in the first place?

How did you find him?

Was he really a customer for what you sell?

Did you quote because he really had a need, or because he wanted to shut you up?

What evidence had you that he had the money available to buy now?

Had he dealt with a competitor before?

Who got the order that time?

Had he got something the customer needed and you had not — or did not find out about?

Were you just a check on market price?

If so, why couldn't you show him more benefits in dealing with you?

Did you just quote for what he asked for, or what you found out he needed?

What feedback did you get from all the staff you spoke to during the survey?

As you went over the details with him, did you listen to what he was saying?

When your written proposition went in, did it show the benefits to him of the equipment, or just the specification and price?

Did you get the right method of acquisition — purchase, rental, hire purchase, leasing?

Did you let him get cold and miss out on follow up?

Would you have bought the scheme yourself, if you'd been him?

Was there conflict on design or anything else between you and the prospect of your own staff, that was pushed to one side or stamped on rather than resolved?

Could you genuinely answer every objection he raised?

Did you prove the answers?

Did you ask him why he did not buy?

Selling Process:

Sales representative introduces
self to new potential client

↓

Ask questions which identifies
clients needs and problems

↓

Translate problems into possible
profitable services

↓

Locate decision makers and
others in the decision making unit

↓

Adapt sales approach to different
interests of key executives

↓

Always identifies appropriate
stage of decision process

↓

Describe service feature
in terms of customer benefits

↓

Encourage a 'creeping commitment'
from the client

Write job description:

    job title
        job holder
        reports to
        date
        job location
        authorities
        responsibilities
        staff reporting

Recruit:

    existing staff
    recommendations
    advertisements
    consultants
    head hunters
    local radio

Answering applicants:

    reject unsuitable
    check references — telephone
                         letter

Offer letter:

   salary
      hours of work
      enclose contract of employment
      holiday arrangements

Interview:

    psychological tests
    work history
    education
    family
    domestic situation
    financial situation
    health
    reasons for leaving

Making final choice rate candidates as follows:

    meets requirements — recommend
    better than average
    marginal
    poor — reject

Plan your sales calls ahead — at least one week

Distribute planned sales calls to colleagues

Spread type of calls — surveys, demonstrations and follow up quotations — evenly through the week

Keep up-to-date records on all customers

Do you know:

    proper name of company?
    affiliations in a group?
    credit rating?
    name of executive level contact?
    type of business?
    number of employees?
    have you ever made a survey or presented a proposal?
    if so for what application
    is there any competitive equipment in use?
    if so for what application?
    for what area of use do you want your equipment considered
    what items will you use to give backing to your case?
    what are the benefits your equipment offers this prospect
    what experience stories of similar instllations will you use?
    have you sufficient examples, illustrations etc?
    what objections do you anticipate?
    have you at least one logical answer to each anticipated objection?
    what will you leave with the prospect to stimulate interest after you have gone?

Use the call reports to prepare accurate sales forecasts covering the next three months by establishing:

    which customers will make repeat orders?
    how much business will come from each customer?
    how many calls will be made during the period?
    performance ratios and average order values?

Selling can be broken down into two main headings — Product Knowledge and Selling Techniques

Product knowledge — the knowledge
  what the product/s is/are?
  what it does, how it works: benefits to the customer?
  where it can be applied?
  who is likely to buy it?
  what is our sales policy?
  how much does it cost, what are the margins
  what is the competition?

Selling techniques — the skill
  territory planning:
    calculating and balancing workload
    plotting the customers
    segmenting the territory
    prepared and using a journey plan

  how industries buy:
    who buys?
    when?
    why?
    how?
  characteristics of the markets:
    prospecting
    researching
    telephoning
    cold calling
  preparing for and starting the sales interview
    identifying the customer's needs
    using questions
    selling benefits
    dealing with objections
    closing the sale
    using sales aids
    presentation techniques
    record-keeping procedures
    feeding back marketing information

This should give information:

  about product
  relevant to customer
  about satisfied customers
  utilise experience professional help
  at very beginning

Catalogues
  can they be combined from data sheets?

Sales publications — define the following:

  who are we talking to?
  what do we want to achieve?
  what evidence do we already have?
  what new facts/opinions do we have?
  what objective evidence can we offer?

Prestige publications

  must avoid introversion and self-congratulation

Production of literature:

input
↓
planning
↓
copywriting
↓
designing
↓
artwork
↓
setting
↓
platemaking
↓
proofs
↓
printing

Note: for International literature there is a language problem and if it is very technical do not attempt to translate

3.21 SALES PROMOTIONS

Sales promotion should concentrate intensively on target groups already influenced by advertising:

    information
    consultation
    stimulation
    sales aids

Trade:

    incentives
    discounts
    free gifts
    competitions
    free offers

Consumer:

    discounts
    2 for the price of 1
    branded packs
    offers
    coupons
    special demonstrations
    free samples
    point of sale

Industrial:

    demonstrations
    exhibitions
    catalogues
    price lists
    technical leaflets
    display units
    'trade in' terms
    free gifts

3.22 IMPROVING PROFITABILITY AND PRODUCTIVITY

Short term

Evaluate products

Detailed appraisal

Set pricing policy

Consider the discount policy

Combat price competition
by raising or lowering prices

Long term planning

Increase   Planning of
Sales volume   products

Effect of product mix on profits

A company can make no more profit than its maximised product mix will allow

The practical criteria for evaluating products have reference to:

    market share
    the relevance of each product to the rest of the range
    the sales volume of the product
    the degree to which capital or other scarce resources are committed to the product, such as management or machine time
    the importance of the product to customers
    its vulnerability, in terms of markets, supplies or costs, to the impact of inflation or government or labout action
    sales forecasting/production planning, difficulties, short runs, etc
    its influence on credit, customer discounts or bad debts
    its impact upon company reputation
    the growth prospects in the market
    its coverage of overhead

the degree to which it ties up sales or service time

its impact upon costs such as waste, breakage, sales commissions

its market acceptance

market competition

These questions will lead to other more detailed appraisals:

How much could be gained by product modification or value analysis?

How far can the price be increased dramatically or the product quality be degraded, or both, either as a prelude to abandonment or in place of it?

How much could be gained by modifying the marketing and sales strategy?

How good are the alternative opportunities in this product area?

How much useful management time and resource can be gained by dropping the product?

How much in total monetary revenue is the product contributing beyond its direct costs, minus any indirect costs which are incurred marketing, selling and distributing this product specifically?

How much is the sale of this product contributing to the sale of other products in this range?

Has the market got potential for the future and, if so, what?

Long term planning of products and mix:

For long term planning purposes the following questions need to be asked:

When is the company likely to face situations of product shortage either because of materials supply or the disruption of production? How extensive are the situations likely to be?

How will competition attempt to reduce total demand, how do they allocate scarce products and how can the company gain a competitive or profitably advantage from this?

What role is played by sales management in deciding how such situations should be handled, and is the special difficulty of the personal selling task at this time recognised?

What are the implications of government policy and special legislation which may be prompted by company policies and which would damage either the market, the supply or long term company profitability?

Increasing sales volume:

cutting the size of the sales force

changing sales methods

improving volume per order

increasing the order to call ratio

increasing price, reducing discounts

lowering customer service levels

concentration upon high-growth, high-profit customers

area expansion

reduction of customer population

change of sales force remuneration, incentives

identifying marginal opportunities for growth

improving sales skills, product, or customer knowledge

key account development

providing sales and customer incentives

Product planning is essential, principles of which are:

To thoroughly measure the likely impact of inflation upon all key markets and products, and to pay close day to day attention to sudden developments

If the operation has to be cut back, cut it back hard though not necessarily fast, but do it earlier rather than later

Offer a tighter, streamlined product range with contingency funds held to exploit sudden opportunities

Develop overseas and other markets which are less prone to inflationary impact. To move from a high fixed cost manufacturing base towards a low fixed cost service organisation is one such option. Service organisations with low capital intensity seem to ride inflation rather better than manufacturing organisations

For new product development, speculate a little, particularly into those areas which do not tie up capital or technical resources and where there is a possibility of a small but fast payback. There are many such opportunities in the market which large companies often ignore because of their small potential size. These become much more attractive in times of zero growth. An acquisition policy towards innovative but small companies may be one answer

Invest at the point when the market is at its most depressed, when some are saying it will become even worse but the company judges it is improving. A high market share, established at the point when the market is depressed, will pay for itself handsomely when substantial volume reappears

Pricing policy:

A pricing policy must take into account a company's freedom to act within the following framework:

dominance of the company's market position
the degree to which substitute products are available
the likelihood of competitive response
the anticipated rise in costs
the degree to which sales and price are related within the chosen market sector
the company's long term business and market objective
the anticipated developments in technology
the need for company growth in sales volume
government restrictions on price
the company's short term profit requirement
relatively small pricing moves which may have a dramatic impact upon profits

Discount policy:

Alongside a sound pricing policy must be a valid and effective discount policy with adequate controls, since:

discounts may fall within pricing regulations
it is harder to reduce a customer's discounts than increase the list price
buyers seek more favourable discount terms when prices go up and play off one supplier against another
additional discounts tends to stay in the customer's pocket rather than being passed through to the end user, hence the market size is not increased
short term and promotional discounts have a tendency to become firmly established as standard discount
standard discounts for bulk orders or for rapid payments or for turnover volume have a tendency to be claimed, even when the conditions under which they are offered are not met

Criteria for combating price competition:

a lower price, and make a charge for delivery or for after sales service
lower prices for bulk orders delivered less frequently
lower prices against guaranteed orders over a period, paid in advance, or in stages
lower prices for sole supplier rights
reciprocal deals, with products and services being exchanged

Guide lines for altering product or service prices

Upwards:

Raise prices when everyone else does
Avoid too frequent price rises
Provide a short moratorium on the price increase for key customers
Provide advance notice of the price increase allowing customers to stock up at old prices
Offer some economy at the same time — a price reduction on small selling items — a promotional short term discount, and so on
Make a good case for the price increase, e.g. cost increases the lift in price, and also demonstrate how the company's productivity or profit improvement programme has helped to absorb some of the increase
Show customers how they can change their buying pattern to minimise the effect of the increase
Introduce a new lower price, lower quality version of the product
Offer alternative payment or service terms

Downwards:

Cut the price when the competition is quiet, or preferably when they are raising their prices
Make the price cut deep enough. It has to be deep enough to overcome the normal inertia

of the market and to 'pay' a buyer for his trouble in considering a new supplier

Do it without notice and promote it very widely. Be careful not to stock load large customers before-hand

Do it only when the price cut can be sustained for a long time, preferably when competition will have great difficulty in meeting it

Never do it unless the market is demonstrably price sensitive

Never do it as a crisis measure when profits are low and the market is turning down, competitors will copy to survive, and a price or discount war will result

Do it on selected loss leading lines, with other products trailed at normal prices

Cost control exists to ensure that actual costs correspond to planned costs. Information and action are central to effective cost control.

Cost control is quite a different actitivity to cost reduction and the two must not be confused.

Ensure that specific promotional plan is produced and adhered to:

> decide role
> set up co-ordination team

Pre-exhibition press contact:

> master press list
> press releases (translations)
> feature articles
> press conferences

Pre-exhibition advertising:

> single insertions do not represent value for money
> consider loose inserts
> general invitation cards

Obtain lists of people to meet from:

> commercial post
> local associations
> Chambers of Commerce
> directories
> overseas agents
> direct mail lists

Produce 1st, 2nd, 3rd category lists:

> most important potentials
> people who influence or make purchases
> balance of master list

Keep exhibition stand in public view through:

> editorial mentions
> press review
> regular press coverage during exhibition
> special events on stand (films, seminars and receptions)

Use personal contacts and direct mail to get listed people to the stand

Organise effective stand supervision for visitors

Have adequate supplies of information on hand for visitors

Apart from direct selling medium of exhibition use it as general promotional medium

After close of exhibition ensure adequate exploitation of follow up

Co-ordination team:
>   report to high enough level
>   allocate own budget
>   split down cost centres
>   utilise outside help (e.g. design and layout)
>   check competitors' activities
>   decide on press contact
>   allocate advertising space
>   list of people who will probably attend
>   set sales, service and information targets
>   train staff who will be on stand helping visitors
>   organise publicity for use on stand
>   set up separate public relations team to maximise results from the exhibition/trade fair

Is it the right exhibition theme?

Should we promote country, product or company?

Should we run our own exhibition/show as an adjunct?

Is there a registration system for subsequent follow up?

Can we invite influential people to our stand?

If we have exhibited there before, what proportion of target audience reached and what was cost per visitor?

The following printed material should be produced:

>   show leaflet identifying:
>   exhibitors
>   exhibits
>   companies participating
>   major products
>   plan of exhibits
>   VIP invitations
>   general invitations or tickets
>   special press release header

Stand design — use creative design consultants to design stand and recognised stand builders to erect stand:
>   portability afterwards
>   total size required
>   image to be presented
>   durability
>   use of area within stand

3.25 ANALYSIS OF EXHIBITION AND TRADE FAIR RESULTS

First analyse all requests or messages into the main action groups:

sales
service
information
other

Then check following:

visitor buying power
composition and competence of stand team
competitor's exhibits
quality for overall exhibition
opportunities for publicity
public relation opportunities

Consider mailings of selected people who:
visited exhibition
asked for tickets
visited your stand

Check overall expenditure:
travel
hotel
entertainment
space cost
stand building cost
publicity

Compare sales with previous exhibitions/trade fair

Check sales achieved against targeted sales

Organise moratorium to be attended by stand personnel/co-ordination team/senior management/other interested people

Check original cost budgets against actual and analyse and explain variances

See Also

4 Manufacture

The following questions need to be asked:

Do adequate standards exist?

Are performance records adequate?

Are variances promptly reported and fully investigated?

If some employees perform both direct and indirect activities, is the system for distinguishing the time spent on each adequate?

Are all processing operations necessary?

Could alternative processes be used to advantage?

Could existing processes be simplified?

Is the sequence of operations the best possible?

Is idle time between operations at a minimum?

Can operations be performed in different departments to avoid handling delays?

Do any operations result in excessive rejects?

Are required completion dates shown on production orders?

In scheduling production is sufficient lead time allowed to enable the accumulation of small orders?

Do we minimize set up costs by allowing sufficient lead time?

Could we schedule labour more efficiently with long production lead times?

Are we sure that special processing requirements can be fitted in, with a sufficiently small lead time?

Are alternative processing methods developed and used for scheduling standard operations in bottleneck areas?

Are cost differences between alternate processing methods known?

Are machine loadings used for production scheduling?

Are workloads planned sufficiently far in advance to permit work force and machines to be balanced?

How much idle time and overtime occurred in the previous period/year?

How much was anticipated?

How much subcontracting was done last year?

Why was this required?

Is scrap/spoilage a significant element of production cost?

Is there a sound procedure for disposing of scrap?

Is scrap sold on the basis of bids?

Are records of spoilage maintained for control purposes?

Are all categories of cost in the manufacturing sphere planned in advance?

Are these the specified responsibility of named individuals?

Does the company employ a flexible budgeting procedure?

Is the inventory of maintenance spares adequate?

Are shortages excessive in the light of the total investment?

General questions that need to be asked:

Are quotations obtained from a number of sources?

Are alternative suppliers approached?

Are all purchase requisitions/purchase orders properly authorised?

Does a policy exist for inviting bids/estimates /tenders?

Are safeguards in existence to prevent the purchasing of excessive quantities?

Is the purchasing department given a sound forecast of materials and other requirements in good time to enable them to be bought on favourable terms?

Are some components currently being made that could be bought from outside at less cost?

ordering costs against stock-holding costs?

Do buyers have the authority to speculate in commodity markets?

Financial questions that need to be asked:

What are the vendors' financial and credit ratings?

What credit terms are offered?

How do these compare with other suppliers' credit terms?

How do they compare with the suppliers' cash flow needs?

What are the cost implications of overdue deliveries?

Are make or buy studies undertaken?

Are the prices competitive (given quality levels)?

What controls do suppliers have over their activities?

Is standard costing employed?

Is sufficient information available by specific cost element to know the reasonableness of the price quoted?

Might past termination or redetermination data be helpful in analysing this procurement?

Is the price reasonable in terms of competition?

What is the suppliers current financial position as shown in the most recent balance sheet?

What is the suppliers current and projected levels of business?

Are there additional sources of capital if they are needed (for the supplier)?

What type of accounting system is employed — job cost? standard cost? other?

Price breakdowns by cost element on fixed price contracts should be furnished

Is there any objection to contracting on other than a fixed price basis?

Is cost accumulated by lot release, and how are initial production costs estimated?

Is special tooling being purchased separately?

Are there any mating interchangeability problems?

Should tooling be coded?

Have we distinguished between special tooling required for the contract and facility items?

How are labour costs accounted for?

Are operations covered by time standards? If so, how are they established?

Does he employ learning curves in projecting labour costs? If so, what rate of learning does he employ?

Are learning curves employed in projecting labour costs? If so, what rate of learning are employed?

Are suppliers employees unionised? If so, when do union contracts expire?

Will designated individuals in engineering, production, and finance be specified from whom the buyer can obtain pertinent information and data as he requires it?

Are all necessary activities included?

Check realistic control points and flow-times have been established

Has he balanced loads among activities so that production will proceed without delay?

Are there any special handling, packaging or shipping requirements that may delay delivery?

Are spares involved, and are they allowed for in the vendor's plans and schedules?

Are all inspection, test, and engineering requirements fully understood?

Is the item adequately described on the blueprints specification, purchase order etc?

Are there any special test or quality control requirements the vendor must meet?

Does he fully understand them, and does he have the time, facilities and know-how to comply?

Are sources accustomed to manufacturing this item?

Do they demonstrate ability to meet this schedule?

Do their past rejection experiences demonstrate ability to meet test and quality requirements?

Is a performance bond advisable?

Should the right be obtained to use or acquire tooling, designs, materials to manufacture the item in case of default?

Are supply costs of consumable production materials properly isolated from general maintenance costs?

Are supplies purchased in economic quantities?

Are there safeguards against overstocking?

Do excessive material shortages arise?

Are obsolete supplies disposed of?

Is there adequate protection against pilferage and wastage?

Are containers compatible with storage, and materials handling?

Is the most suitable materials handling equipment used?

Can materials be moved best by gravity or on rollers?

Is a conveyor justified?

Are fork-lift trucks and pallets used to advantage?

Are the materials handling and manufacturing functions effectively co-ordinated?

Where should in-coming and out-going materials be located with respect to work stations?

Can operations be combined at one work station to reduce materials handling?

Are containers uniform to permit stacking?

Can pallatised loads be used?

Could lighter or low cost packaging be used?

Is shrink wrapping possible with current advance in technology?

Is packaging design co-ordinated with materials handling?

Do all items really need packages?

Are scrap and waste materials dealt with effectively

Are containers marked/coloured for easier segregation/identification?

Could materials be purchased in sizes or quantities that would make for easier materials handling?

How much capital is tied up in obsolete materials/components?

Could excess stocks be sold in bulk with special discounts, or is it cheaper to allow high stocks to run down through normal usage?

How much of inventory investment is in work-in-progress?

What are the costs of carrying each type of inventory?

What are the costs of reordering items for inventory?

Are order points developed for each item on the basis of lead times, rates of usage, and safety stocks?

If of value, are returnable containers properly accounted for and controlled?

Could a deposit system be used for returnable containers/pallets?

Are incoming goods examined for quantity, quality and conformance to order?

Has an analysis been carried out to verify lead times used in reordering?

Where sales are seasonal is it more advisable to produce in accordance with demand, or to produce at an even rate, and use stocks as a buffer?

Who are the key people in the vendor's organisation?

What are their titles and functions?

What is the average experience and educational level in each department of group?

What are the vendor's design and development procedures?

How does he incorporate design changes?

How does he integrate tooling and manufacturing techniques with research and development activities?

Will he comply with the buyer's engineering standards and procedures for items made to buyer design, and will he produce drawings on buyer format when he requests it?

What are the vendor's inspection procedures and controls?

How frequently does he calibrate tools, gauges, and test equipment for meeting primary engineering standards?

How does he control test equipment furnished to subcontractors?

Does he have a separate Reliability Engineering or Quality Control function?

Where does it report, and how is it organised?

What is the scope of its activity?

What is the nature of the planning, scheduling, and inventory control systems?

How are requirements released — by job, by lot, by forecast?

How is production performance reported (actual versus scheduled)?

Who is production performance reported by and is the level high enough to ensure few problems?

Can the frequency of performance reporting be increased to limit possible future problems?

How does the vendor control and incorporate engineering changes?

Who is responsible for machine and manpower loading?

Does the vendor forecast loads, and is there a procedure for comparing current loads against forecast?

What is his system of stock and material control?

How does he identify and separate materials?

How does he dispose of scrap, surplus and obsolete materials?

What are his procedures of in-process inspection and quality control?

What is the procedure of receiving inspection?

Does he require certifications or test approvals from his suppliers? If so, for what items of purchase?

Are spares involved? If so, are they allowed for in plans and schedules?

What are the quality control arrangements?

Financial checks on supplier's capability:
    use credit reference agency
    inspect previous balance sheets
    bank/accountants references
    trade references
    individual references on Directors
    check credit terms offered
    ask other buyers

Decentralised v Centralised Purchasing

Decentralised purchasing:
        faster reaction time
        awareness of local conditions
        closer to plant management
        better if many product lines
        tight delivery times
        large company with separate divisions

Centralised purchasing:
        strong control
        economies of bulk purchase

Note: Decentralised purchasing can only succeed with a good structural management system
Centralised purchasing if imposed on a completely decentralised company will not work because divisions will want to keep their own autonomy

Discounts:
    always ask for discount
    take discount if offered even if terms of payment are not strictly adhered to
    check to see if other suppliers (or even divisions within own suppliers company) offer discounts
    offer prompt payment if discount offered (after goods delivered)

4.6 VALUE IMPROVEMENT

Manufacturer v Customer

- improved product design without changing quality or use
- material substitutions
- better productions methods
- lowered material costs by better price negotiations
- removes unnecessary characteristics, both functional and quality

- reduced product price but no quality and functional use
- improved product quality
- additional characteristics to improve functional use

Value improvement can be achieved under the following main headings:

Price analysis:
- best possible price while still allowing a reasonable profit
- identify elements of highest costs to incite improvement action on the vendor's part
- identify any possible hidden charges or unnecessary cost factors
- detect any poor specifications that increase costs and price

Procurement research:
- Analysis of trends of cost and usage
  - better buying plans
  - specification changes
  - reduced shortages because of co-ordinated buying

Design analysis';
- using purchasing knowledge
- using vendor feedback

4.7 PURCHASING EFFECTIVENESS REPORTS

Progress reports can cover:

- Reduced vendor prices through negotiations
- Improved practise — blanket ordering, systems purchasing, order consolidation
- Savings — e.g. tooling costs, freight charges, cash discounts
- Substitutions of less costly material
- Quantity discounts
- Phased-out deliveries, and/or economical ordering quantities
- Standardised material or better parts specifications enabling less costly material use or more choice of vendors
- Using close suppliers, to reduce warehouse space used
- Better packaging, palletised purchases, re-usable/lighter containers
- New buying sources
- Recommendations on changing from buying to making, or making to buying
- Taking advantage of price fluctuations
- Simplifying systems and procedures:
  - eliminated excess forms
  - eliminated unneeded records
  - simplified order writing
  - grouped orders
  - gave better service or information
- Better warranties
- Increases revenue in sales of obsolete, surplus or damaged material

Purchasing effectiveness:

- Ratio of Purchasing to total company personnel
- Purchasing department cost per £ of purchase
- Actual v budgeted cost
- £ savings per £ of purchase
- Variance of actual material cost to standard
- Cost of material
- Cost per Purchase Order
- Number of transactions handled
- % of deliveries late
- % of returned shipments to total
- £'s of discounts earned

4.8 DESIGN REQUIREMENTS

Preliminaries:

    feasibility
    suitability
    composition of product
    aesthetics

Materials:

    economy
    purity
    availability
    quality

    Note: could we use new types of materials?

Physical aspects:

    fatigue
    vibration
    shock
    wear
    corrosion
    damp
    dirt

General factors to consider:

    could standard parts be used for the design?
    have we considered the product's future environment?
    what reliability will the customer accept?
    has the ease of manufacture been considered?
    what type of quality control will be required?
    will assembly be easy and cheap?
    what difficulties will there be for routine maintenance and repair?
    is our product up to the general standards of design from competitors?
    will we maximise the design potential (eg Design Council awards) for public relation purposes

4.9 MAKE OR BUY ANALYSIS

Quantifiable factors:

    raw material costs
    scrap percentages as they affect material and labour costs
    learning costs at the start of production
    freight in and incoming inspection on both raw material and purchased parts
    labour needed
    fringe benefit costs on labour
    additional overhead:
        depreciation
        maintenance costs
        spare parts
    tooling costs
    power fuel costs
    additional supervision
    inventory carrying costs
    additional space
    money tied up in space saving equipment
    material handling costs
    plant capacity
    spare factory space availability

Non-quantifiable factors:

    additional/lessened burden on supervision and higher management
    quality and delivery performance of vendors
    need for an assured source
    need to safeguard designs or process secrets
    aim of employment stability
    possession of needed skills
    raw material availability
    foreseeable and suspected technological change
    effect on existing suppliers and their relationship to the purchaser
    government reaction
    trade union involvement
    involvement of outside countries and foreign government
    press reaction

4.10 INVENTORY MANAGEMENT

The major factors in inventory acquisition are:

Purchased parts:
>   purchasing department costs
>   freight inwards
>   receiving department costs
>   incoming inspection
>   portion of warehouse labour involved in putting away
>   personnel involved in accounts payable

Manufactured parts:
>   set-up labour
>   start-up material and/or scrap
>   first piece and later inspection
>   cost of preparing a manufacturing order

Inventory carrying costs elements are:

>   insurance
>   taxes
>   space
>   material handling
>   return on investment
>   physical inventorying
>   loss, damage and deterioration
>   obsolescence
>   economic trends
>   optional miscellaneous items:
>>   record keeping and accounting
>>   management charges

Economic Order Quantity:

Balance cost of placing order to cost of inventory holding =

$$\frac{\text{Annual usage (£'s) x Cost placing order}}{\text{Cost of holding material}}$$

4.11 EDP IN PURCHASING

Possible savings:

>   removes routine work
>   enables orders to be consolidated
>   data enables better negotiation
>   measure of work load
>   purchase progress report initiated or improved
>   small orders can be highlighted

To determine the design requirements of any electronic data processing system, consider the following:

>   number of different items ordered per year
>   number of different transactions per year
>   amount of money spent per item per year
>   price quotations by item and supplier
>   price history record by item
>   list of current suppliers for any given item or group of items
>   categorise items by value, i.e. A-B-C analysis
>   calculate economic order quantity and compare with price break points
>   generate the purchase order upon stock depletion below an indicated point
>   check vendor's order acknowledgment
>   list open orders — by buyer, by due date, and in total
>   note receipt of material against the order
>   compare invoices with receiving report and with the order, and print the check, if they agree
>   vendor performance on delivery and quality

Consider the use of:
>   in house data processing staff to write programme
>   outside time sharing bureau
>   ready made 'off the shelf' package

Failure costs:

> scrap
> rework
> reinspection
> sorting of rejects
> losses on sale of substandard items
> servicing of customers' complaints
> extra operations
> selective assembly
> downtime
> after sales service (under guarantee or warranty)
> lost sales opportunities

Appraisal costs:

> incoming materials
> manufacturing processes
> products at all stages of manufacture and use
> storage facilities
> gauges and measuring devices

Prevention costs:

> special investigations into failure costs
> training personnel in control of quality
> provision of quality reports

Note: The loss of turnover in terms of lost customer goodwill can far outweigh the extra quality controls costs or customer basic service expenditure

Are quality control standards for all materials, components and products regularly reviewed?

Are tolerances, allowances, finish, and other requirements necessary and appropriate?

Can the specification requirements be raised to improve quality without increasing cost?

Will lowering the specification requirements reduce costs significantly without the loss of quality?

Can quality be improved by using new processes?

Will a change in inspection requirements affect the rate (hence cost) of rejects?

Is defective work excessive?

Are causes of defective work noted?

Is product performance in the field evaluated?

Could quality control costs be reduced (without sacrificing quality) by reducing or eliminating some inspection procedures?

Is the company paying for costly inspection at other sources when these could be more economically performed at the company's own premises?

Are inspection activities scheduled in such a way that they do not hold production up?

Are quality control ideas applied throughout the company rather than being confined to the production sphere?

Do the benefits from using quality control procedures exceed their cost?

Could work study be used to identify area with least (and most) problems regarding quality control?

If areas of least and most can be identified how can some cross fertilisation of ideas and practices be best effected?

4.14 SAMPLING METHODS

How large a sample should be inspected?

How should the items in the sample chosen for inspection be selected from the total?

When the number of defective items in the sample has been determined how can the number of defective items in the total be estimated?

What is the possible or probable percentage of error in the estimate of the total number of defective items?

What percentage of defective items in the sample is sufficient to justify the rejection of the entire lot?

How can the number of defective items in various samples be charted over time in order that unfavourable trends may be detected and the causes corrected?

Consider the use of time saving terminals linked to large frame computers for the following:
instant results
choice of methods
most accurate answer
ongoing availability to update with new data
new and different programmes always available

4.15 LOCATION OF NEW PLANT

Main considerations:

proximity to raw materials
fuel and power availability and cost
transportation
labour supply
water supply
water and disposal facilities
accommodation
pollution

Less important:

market location
living and social conditions
proximity to suppliers
plant maintenance services

Site conditions:

topography (flat, cheap or zoned, land, sea, lake or river location)
soil condition
water supply
waste disposal
position of plant to local transport facilities
availability of homes for workers
local by-laws, including sanitation air and stream pollution
living conditions for labour and management; climate, scenery, recreational facilities, schools, churches, public transport
community directives for zoning house use and community attitudes towards manufacturing activity

Location — further factors:

political climate, risk of nationalisation
integrity of Government controls etc.
taxation implications
government grants and common market aid

Factors governing the locating of industry and the relation of new development sites are divided between physical and social elements

The meaning of risk:

> uncertainty creates risk
> risk is the consequence of bad chance
> reducing the uncertainty through better information does not of itself reduce the risk
> the risk in any project may not be a true measure of the risk to an organisation of undertaking the project
> risk is what you stand to lose less what you can afford to lose

Sources of risk:

> risk from insufficient numbers
> risk from misinterpretation
> risk from bias
> risk from external change
> risk from errors of analysis

Analysis of risk:

> risks may be classified according to the way in which they affect forecasting earning power by understating the outlay
> complete failure to break through to the objective
> schedule slippage
> shortening the economic life
> reducing the rate of increase of income
> failing to synchronise with availability of funds

Risk can either be:
> controlled
> not controlled but influenced
> neither controlled nor influenced, but quantified

Funds requirement for any new project
> new product development
> prototype manufacture and testing
> financing production plant
> providing factory space
> financing stocks of raw materials and components
> initial sales promotion
> stocks in the distribution chain
> losses during the market development phase
> increase in debtor investment after product launch

Protection of critical areas:

> enclosed by physical barriers
> limited access
> guard force on duty
> locks
> intrusion detection devices
> key control system
> package and material control system

Fire protection:

> regulations posted and enforced?
> alarm system in all areas?
> how fast is local Fire Dept.?
> secondary water supply available?
> how much equipment available?
> do you have fire and rescue squads?
> proper storage of combustible material?
> proper training in use of equipment?
> do you have fire drills?
> do you read the Fire Insurance Inspection reports?

Bomb Threats:

> proper channels of communication including reporting procedures
> liaison with law enforcement
> liaison with medical and first aid facilities
> fire procedure
> evacuation procedure
> search procedure
> area to be protected
> determination of company liability in the event of no evacuation
> what factors will weigh in the decision to evacuate or not evacuate?
> post reporting procedures
> procedure to go into effect if there actually is a bomb explosion

Limiting effects of blast:
> wire netting
> bomb curtains (nets) for glass windows
> sand bags/blankets for letter bombs
> X-ray machines for suspicious parcels

4.18 INDUSTRIAL SECURITY

General points:

> try to control talking
> destroy carbons
> use special paper
> develop internal alarms
> special conference room
> watch special visitors
> daytime clearing of classified areas
> electronic devices
> false information

Profile of a 'Secret Stealer'

sudden acquisition of wealth
> possible scandal or rumour surrounding him
> chronic complainer
> heavy drinker or alcoholic
> compulsive gambler
> mentally disturbed
> criminal background
> extensive debts
> narcotics user

Can a recognised security organisation be used to check for bugs in high risk area?

Is disposal of security waste (eg computer print outs) monitored?

Are paper shredders used where possible?

Should security guards be employed to check entrances into building/factory?

See Also

5 Distribution and Storage

5.1 WAREHOUSE CONTROL PROCEDURES

Incoming:

> check against documents received
> issue goods received note
> quality control — endorse goods received note

Outgoing:

> check against documents

Order processing

Edit order:
> identify customer
> establish products required
> check delivery date

Record order:
> establish account number
> establish delivery area
> acknowledge order

Credit Control:
> **check credit limit**
> **establish credit outstanding**

Allocate stock:
> notify customer if delay

Retain order until:
> goods available
> delivery due
> van run due

Vehicle route
> **advice transport section**
> **arrange most cost effective delivery routing**

Picking lists:
> reverse sequence of delivery of goods

Customer delivery notes:
> date of delivery
> signature

5.2 WAREHOUSE OPERATING EFFICIENCY

Space utilisation efficiency is:

ratio of cubic area occupied to net space available (net — gross space less clearances, stairwells, service facilities)

> could more space be obtained?
> is layout poor with too many aisles?
> would racks help?
> **could goods be stored at work stations?**
> **if so, is all the height available being used?**
> can bulk storage be improved?
> is there a storage plan for each area?
> is warehouse tidy and well stacked?
> re-examine aisles:
>> any unnecessary aisles?
>> if so, how many and where?
>> can they be eliminated or shortened?
>> are aisles in the right places?
>> and laid out for maximum use?
>> **where and how can aisle width be reduced?**
>> **can trucks, stacker cranes be used?**

Handling characteristics:

> ease of handling and stacking
> long materials
> sheet materials
> susceptibility to damage, contamination, infestation
> **special requirements of temperature:**
> humidity

The storage modules adopted are also important. Possible methods include:

> single parts, cartoned or loose
> outer cases, bag and sacks
> **boxes**
> unit loads, pallets and sub-containers
> freight containers
> loose solids and liquids in less than unit loads

Packaging:

>   the duration and type of journey involved, and the strains involved
>   the fragility or perishability of the goods transported
>   the handling and stacking methods which will be employed at each change in mode
>   the sensitivity of the goods to environment
>   the unit value of the goods and how much packaging can be afforded
>   the extent to which the goods have to be packaged for other reasons
>   the likelihood of the goods contaminating other goods
>   the need for identification
>   the desirability of not having to break down the package for final consignment
>   the desirability of separate items arriving together at the destination
>   border documentation and customs requirements
>   the need to stop pilfering
>   limitations imposed by doors, hatches, cranes
>   statutory requirements — e.g. rail packaging regulations, IATA rules
>   insurance requirements

Routing and scheduling:

>   number and type of call
>   capacity of vehicle and vehicle type
>   urbanisation and vehicle speeds obtainable
>   balance between driving time and delivery time
>   size of orders
>   distance between calls
>   depot location
>   maximum working day
>   shop or customer opening hours
>   road network
>   opportunities for return loads
>   load layout and use of compartments for different products
>   maintenance of an adequate service level

Logistic Factors

>   volume of goods, inwards and outwards
>   regular deliveries or movements and frequencies
>   variable deliveries — variants and seasonal effects
>   trends — increasing or diminishing
>   customers' expectation of service
>   type of movement — factory to warehouse, first or second degree outlet or export

Equipment Groups:

>   manual equipment
>   sack trucks
>   stillage trucks
>   pallet trucks
>   fixed route equipment
>   chutes
>   conveyors
>   sorting systems
>   unitised systems
>   pallet trucks
>   fork lift trucks
>   stacker crane

Stock location:

>   **fixed location — bin storage, but this can waste space**
>   **random location — least unoccupied space, but increases search time**
>   **zoned location — fixed or random located within zones**

Manning of warehouse:

>   evaluate operating requirements of warehouse
>   study systems and improve where possible
>   construct job descriptions
>   perform work study exercise
>   implement recommendations and improve operating methods
>   develop incentive schemes where necessary

5.4 PHYSICAL DISTRIBUTION FACILITIES AUDIT

Is the cost per unit changing rapidly on the following:
- transport
- trunking
- local delivery
- warehouse
- local depot
- break-bulk point
- stockholding
- If so, why?

Has the distribution workload (delivery size etc.) changed in level or composition?

Are there changes in technology and environment which upset or challenge the economic basis of the distribution system?

Does the measurement of delivery service show the company to lag behind competition?

Is the company losing sales because of this?

What do our surveys of customer opinion show?

5.5 PHYSICAL DISTRIBUTION FACILITIES

Are depots needed?
If so, how many and where?
How large and with what facilities?
Are central warehouses needed?
If so, how many and where?
How large and with what facilities?
expanded as trade grows
Lease v purchase?
How many types of vehicle should be used?
What ancillary equipment should they have?
How many vehicles of each type are required?
How many spare trailers are required for each type of vehicle?
What garaging and workshop facilities are required?
Where should they be located?
What products should be distributed through the system?
Should raw materials, semi-finished goods, supplies, bought-in items, be distributed through the warehouses?
What customers should receive their orders through the system?
What unit-load handling policy should be adopted?
Should the system make use of trunking?
Which products should be stocked in which warehouses and/or depots?
Which customers should receive their orders from which depots?
Should they be served from more than one depot?
Which customers should receive their orders direct from a warehouse or factory?
Under what circumstances could other customers receive their orders direct?
Which warehouses should be supplied from which factories?
Which depots should be supplied from which warehouses and/or factories?

Under what circumstances, if at all, should the warehouses be used as 'shunt' or transit warehouses?

What frequency of service should customers receive?

What minimum order-to-delivery interval should the customers be allowed?

Types of distribution methods:

Rail:
    own trucks
    British Rail trucks

Road:
    company fleet
    leased fleet
    contract fleet
    individual carriers

Canal:
    barges

Ships:
    purchase
    contract

Air:
    contract

What combinations of the above give best distribution methods?

How many types of different means should be used to maximise cost effectiveness

The average volume of goods demanded by product and geographical location

The marginal profit associated with the sale of the various products after allowing for all other marginal costs *except* distribution

The expected growth in product demand

The seasonal or other cyclical character of the product demands

The random day-to-day fluctuations in the product demands

The physical characteristics of products

The number and location of factories

The number and geographical location of customers to be delivered to

The ordering behaviour of customers including the frequency and size of orders

The cost characteristics of road transport, including capital costs, mileage dependent running costs, standing charges and other time dependent costs, and their dependence on whether the vehicles are owned, leased, contracted or short-term hired

The physical characteristics of possible vehicles, including, in particular, their weight and volume capacities

Distances and times to travel between locations in the system

Loading and/or unloading times at factories, warehouses, depots and customers

The costs of other means of transport

The dependence of transport costs on warehouse and depot facilities and vice versa

One-off costs associated with changing the distribution system

Restrictions on manpower, land and other resources available at the possible warehouse and depot sites and the capacities

Restrictions on capital funds available

The characteristics of the existing system
The uncertainty associated with estimating the value of these factors under future circumstances

Other constraints:
    company policy
    local authorities
    government
    law restrictions
    trade unions
    customers
    competitors
    formal agreements
    informal understandings

Compare costs of company-owned transport function with outside contractors?

Are the best means of transport (cost and service viewpoints) used for different products?

Are increases in transport costs considered to be unavoidable and thus passed on to customers without studying the efficiency of transport activities?

Are *all* transport costs accounted for under the heading of transport?

Can those vehicles having disproportionately high operating costs (in relation to other vehicles of the same make, age, and capacity) be identified?

How are standards set in the transport sphere? (If there are no standards, should they be introduced?)

Is control over fuel exercised by having a bulk storage facility, or does the company rely on outside agencies?

Could the costs be reduced by hiring a fleet (contract or lease) rather than owning vehicles?

Is maintenance planned or available on a crisis basis?

Does the cost control system reveal the extent to which transport facilities are under-utilised?

Does an established procedure exist for scheduling and routing vehicles?

Does routing take into account different road types, urban areas?

Is the most expensive resource (e.g. driver or vehicle) the focus of attention?

Is the capacity constraint of the fleet, volume or weight? (Are right sizes of vehicles in use?)

Can mechanical loading/unloading methods be employed with the type of vehicles in use?

How is performance measured? Which aspects of performance are measured? Driver performance, driver utilisation, vehicle utilisation, delay time

What follow-up results from the extraction of variances?

Who takes responsibility for the cost of special deliveries?

To what extent can use be made of existing forms/reports (such as log sheets, mileage records etc.) in building up costs?

What exceptions should be made to the usual arrangements?

What inter-company movements frequency standards should be adopted?

What vehicle types should work what routes?

What characteristics should the journey patterns and consequent vehicle schedules have?

What should be the maximum time away from base allowed?

What maintenance and replacement policy should be adopted in respect of the vehicles?

During what hours should the depots, warehouses and factory despatch points operate?

On what routes, with which vehicles, and under what circumstances should multiple shift working of the transport fleet take place?

How much staff and labour is required to operate the transport fleet, the warehouses, the depots, the factory despatch points?

What management structure should be adopted?

Where should 'picking and packing' of customers orders take place?

Should different arrangements be made for export orders?

What arrangements should be made for setting stock action levels, and monitoring and allocating stocks?

What arrangements should be made for the physical process of raising customers' orders, acknowledgments, despatch notes etc.?

What other control documentation and procedures are required?

What is the broad specification of the management information system required?

What percentage of total sales for each product is directly transacted with users?

What is the history of the introduction of the product and the sequence of marketing steps which led to its present distribution?

What is the replenishment lead time?

What is the history of "out-of-stock" situations?

What stocks are normally held at the plant? Average or seasonal?

What stocks are normally in the distributive pipeline?

is a new warehouse needed?
how much flexibility is needed in the face of
changed markets and equipment?
how much room for expansion?
old or new premises?
what are the design objectives?

Warehouse design objectives long v short term:

minimise need to extend the building
in the next x years
v
minimise capital expenditure by building
only for present needs

enable changes in the layout to be made easily
and cheaply by having large roof spans
v
minimise capital expenditure by using cheapest
spacing of stanchions

minimise building maintenance costs by using
better, more expensive materials in the
construction
v
minimise capital expenditure by using lower
quality (cheaper) materials

minimise labour costs
v
minimise equipment costs

Site selection:

planning regulations, the availability of
services, electricity, gas, water, waste
disposal, plus repair services for specialised
equipment
the availability of transport, in addition to
road and motorway access, good rail, sea,
or canal services may be needed
the availability of labour
any government controls or special grants
which are applicable
the level of local taxes

Parameters for new building design:

what vehicles are used at present
handling equipment required
manoeuvreability of trucks
deck lights
number loading points
number handling bays
possible use of containerisation

Future changes in vehicles:

size of marshalling area
doorway size (draughtproofing and structural problems if too large)
height — note clearances and stocking
height required
illumination levels
sprinklers
services required (steam, air, electricity,
water, fans etc.)
floor loading — reinforcement, if any
columns — integrate within storage areas, if
possible

5.9 NEGOTIATIONS

Know what you want — both the major and minor objectives of your transaction

Don't play the negotiation 'by ear'

Know what the seller would be satisfied in achieving

Open up the negotiations by a discussion of mutual interest

Avoid making first demands, proposals, or even positive assertions or claims

Negotiation is in a very real sense a test of strength so the buyer should strive to avoid a pattern of concession

Introduce trading points at the outset, i.e. those points that you can concede later

Never give anything away, seek counter-concessions in exchange

Know what limitations are imposed on the seller-negotiator

Don't make the buyer lose face on a point and therefore lose an ally

Seek technical assistance and support where necessary

Admit your own shortcomings and seek help

If negotiations are conducted by a team make sure that all the members are on the same team

In a team let the team leader lead

Always have a dry run with team negotiations

Be sensitive to the emotional temperature of the negotiation — lower the temperature when necessary

Minimise emotional involvement by always sticking to the facts

Avoid hearsay, personal opinion

Be conscious of the psychology of the negotiation

> Give the buyer prestige and importance
> Never argue — be cool, calm and calculating
> Keep your eyes and ears open

5.10 VEHICLE SECURITY PROCEDURES

background check on drivers
saturation of area with guard personnel
internal alarms in truck
meter in truck giving mileage, time, speed
modern freight forms — bills of lading etc.
locking and disabling devices
use of seals
large numbers on roof of truck
secure loading areas
dock surveillance by closed circuit TV
road patrols
check-in points along route
telephone in cab
planted merchandise
secretly labelled objects detected by X-ray
firearms should not be carried by driver

See Also

6 Personnel

6.1 PERSONNEL ACTIVITIES

Manpower planning

Recruitment

Selection

Training
   induction
   on the job
   managerial

Job evaluation

Promotions

Transfers

Redundancies

Short time working

Discipline interviews

Grievance settlements

Personnel records

Wage/Salary policies

Job analysis/evaluation

Loans

Fringe benefits
   life insurance
   health insurance
   accident insurance
   pensions
   share incentives

Safety programmes

Recreational facilities

Canteen facilities

Company housing

Plant security

Company publications

Notice boards

Industrial relations

Charitable donations

Executive development

6.2 ROLE OF THE PERSONNEL FUNCTION

Is the role of the personnel function defined?

Has the organisation developed personnel policies to serve as continuing guide-lines on personnel matters in the following areas:

quality of managers, staff and hourly paid employees

levels of remuneration (pay and fringe benefits compared with market rates, and constant review

amount and scope of training schemes

promotion and the extent to which the organisation intends to rely on promotion from within

employee relations:
   recognition of unions
   the rights of union or employee representatives
   the extent to which employees should be kept informed on and consulted about plans and policies
   the approach used for dealing with disciplinary and grievance problems, including the extent to which appeals can be made and the use of external conciliation or arbitration procedures
   redundancy — the basis for deciding who should be made redundant, the amount of notice, levels of payment and the degree to which prior consultation should take place
   safety, health and welfare the degree to which the organisation wishes to go beyond statutory obligations concerning the health and safety and provide welfare and recreational facilities

Is the personnel function carrying out any activities which more properly should be carried out elsewhere in the organisation?

Is the organisation structure of the personnel function suitable for fulfilling its roles and carrying out its activities?

is the head of the function in a position to exert sufficient influence over the formulation and implementation of personnel policies?

are individuals in positions within the function given explicit information on the main activities that they should carry out?

are individuals given sufficient authority to carry out their duties?

have standards of performance and targets been established wherever possible for members of the function?

is there any overlap between the responsibilities of individuals?

Recommended structure:

Personnel director — responsible to the main board for all aspects of personnel with some or all of the following key people responsible to him:

Personnel manager
Training manager
Security advisor
House journal editor
Canteen manager
Industrial relations advisor

Establish the future need for personnel by number and quality of employees on the basis of the manpower plan

Establish job descriptions for all managerial positions.

Conduct appointment interviews, evaluate candidates. Recommend new appointments to line management.

Develop and administer a wage and salary structure, including salary brackets for each position and with fringe and other benefit packages.

Introduce and service a system of appraisal of all employees by the superior, as a basis for promotion and planning the filling of vacancies.

In conjunction with line management, identify employees suitable as successors to the present management.

Develop and administer internal and external training programmes, so that employees can become familiar with modern methods.

Work out individual training programmes (attendance at courses and seminars, job rotation) for managers and future managers worthy of promotion

Administer all personnel records.

Organise and administer the social programmes

pension fund
life insurance
medical aid
canteen
sports club
insurances

Organise and administer suggestion schemes.

Represent the firm in matters relating to:
> works council
> trade unions
> employment law
> accident prevention
> with assistance from other specialist
> functions

Observe morale in the firm and take steps to keep it as high as possible

Contact with employers' federations and employment officers at universities and colleges.

Limitation of responsibilities:
> The personnel manager is responsible for ensuring that the firm has at all times the right number and quality of employees.
>
> He cannot appoint, dismiss or promote anyone or award any increase in wages or salary without the consent of the line manager concerned.
>
> He cannot make any alterations in the organisation structure of the firm without the consent of the manager concerned.

The salary policies of a company provide the basis upon which its salary structure and salary administration procedures are developed. The main areas are:
> basic philosophy
>> the importance attached by the organisation to the total remuneration package as the means of attracting, motivating and retaining staff
> market rates
>> the extent to which market rates will be allowed to influence the salary structure and the level of salaries within the organisation in relation to market rates
> equity
>> the degree to which the organisation is going to strive after internal pay relativities between jobs will be established and maintained
> reward system
>> the specific role of financial rewards and incentives as part of the reward system
> salary structure
>> the degree to which this should be formalised and the design of the salary structure; that is, the number and width of the salary brackets and the amount of overlap, if any, between salary brackets
> incremental system
>> the use of salary increments to provide rewards
> incentive scheme
>> the use of bonus and profit sharing schemes to provide incentive
> flexibility
>> the amount of discretion that managers will be allowed to fix salary levels for jobs, determine starting rates or award promotional or merit increments
> total remuneration
>> the best mix of basic salary and other benefits
> communication
>> the amount of information given to staff, collectively or individually, about salary policies

Note: Government restrictions

6.5 SALARY ADMINISTRATION

Salary administration procedures are concerned with the implementation and control of salary policies and with the control of salary costs against budgets.

The aims must be:

serve the aims and objectives of the undertaking as a whole

ensure that a sufficient number of suitable people are attracted to join the undertaking

encourage suitable staff to remain in its employment

provide appropriate rewards for good performance and incentives for further improvements in performance

achieve equity in the pay for similar jobs and consistency in the differentials that exist between different levels of jobs in accordance with their relative value

provide not only for fairness in the operation of the salary system but also for staff to be convinced that the system is fair

operate flexibly enough to accommodate changes in the relative market rates for different skills and in the organisation of the undertaking

achieve simplicity in operation as an aid to staff understanding and to minimize administrative effort

ensure that the salary policies are consistent with the requirements of Government and with the public interest

achieve these aims at the least cost to the undertaking

6.6 BASIC FEATURES OF A SALARY STRUCTURE

All jobs are allocated into a salary grade within the structure on the basis of an assessment of their internal and external value to the organisation.

Each salary grade consists of a salary bracket or band. No individuals holding a job in the grade can go beyond the maximum of the salary band unless he or she is promoted.

Jobs can be regarded within the structure when it is decided that their value has altered because of a change in responsibilities or a pronounced movement in the market rate for the job.

General increases in the cost of living or in market rates are dealt with by proportionate increases to the maxima and minima of salary bands.

The salary bands are wide enough to provide room to progress individual salaries in relation to performance and in accordance with the level of the job. At junior clerical levels the band could be no wider than 15 per cent to 20 per cent. At supervisory and managerial levels the bands could be between 35 per cent and 60 per cent but the most typical width is 50 per cent.

A differential between each salary band which provides adequate scope for rewarding increased responsibility on promotion to the next higher grade but does not create too wide a gap between adjacent grades and thus reduce the amount of flexibility available for grading jobs. This should normally be between 15 per cent and 25 per cent but 20 per cent is probably a typical differential.

An overlap between bands which allows very experienced individuals in a grade to be paid more than inexperienced individuals in the next higher grade.

All jobs allocated into a salary grade are assumed to be broadly of the same level. In other words, they normally have the same minimum and maximum rates which correspond with the grade boundaries. If there are any exceptions to this rule in the shape of jobs with a higher minimum or lower maximum salary, they should be specified.

Progression within a grade depends on the performance of the individual. It would generally be assumed that all fully competent individuals in any jobs in a grade would eventually reach the normal maximum of the grade, if they are not promoted out of it. Less competent individuals may stop progressing at some point below the grade maximum. In some circumstances, provision may be made for exceptional individuals to receive more than the normal maximum.

SALARY BANDS

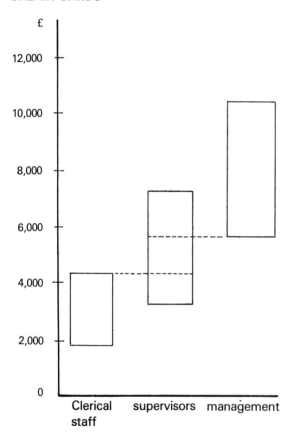

Preference for a fixed rather than a variable system of remuneration related to the following:

the acceptance of a relationship between length of service in a job and value to the organisation, especially in jobs which require a training or probationary period

the fairness of such systems and their freedom from the arbitrary use of management discretion

the mere size and geographical distribution of individual departments, as well as the need, under any system, to keep the standards of granting increments in line, as between one department and another, may present difficulties

the existence of only limited scope for variations in job performance or special difficulties in measuring performance

the motivational value of fixed systems in situations where it is felt to be of primary importance to emphasise teamwork and co-operative attitudes rather than individual competitiveness

the ease with which fixed incremental systems can be administered

the support of fixed systems by the trade unions, who generally believe that pay arrangements should be defined and made explicit to the maximum possible extent and express doubts about the fairness of any incremental scheme which is based on performance assessment

the proven acceptability of the system over a long period

The arguments in favour of variable incremental schemes are as follows:

they provide an effective basis for motivation by relating pay to performance

they allow management discretion in the award of salary increases

they are inherently cost-effective, not simply in the sense of restraining costs but of ensuring that increases are related to assessed contributions

they provide more flexibility to match pay to the individual in the face of greater job mobility and changing conditions

managers prefer to feel that increased effectiveness will bring commensurate rewards

Profit sharing schemes endeavour to achieve one or more of the following objectives:

to encourage employees to identify themselves more closely with the company by developing a common concern for its progress

to stimulate a greater interest amongst employees in the affairs of the company as a whole

to encourage better co-operation between management and employees

to recognise that employees of the company have a moral right to share in the profits they have helped to produce

to demonstrate in practical terms the goodwill of the company towards its employees

Schemes which share profits according to some universal formula amongst all or most employees may not provide any real incentive because they fail to satisfy the three basic requirements of an incentive scheme, namely:

that the reward should bear a direct relation to the effort

that the payment should follow immediately or soon after the effort

that the method of calculation should be simple and easily understood

Types of Schemes:

The main **types** of profit sharing schemes **are:**

immediate cash — a proportion of profits **is paid direct to employees in cash as soon as profits are determined**

immediate shares — profits are distributed **direct to employees in the form of stock as soon as the profits are determined**

deferred cash — profits are credited to employee accounts to be paid at retirement or in other stated circumstances

The amount of reward received after tax should be sufficiently high to encourage staff to accept a high and exacting standard of performance.

Standard bonuses should not be less than ten per cent of the base salary and, if the circumstances demand an effective incentive, the standard bonus should be around 20 to 30 per cent of salary.

The incentive arrangement should, as far as possible, be related to criteria over which the individual has a substantial measure of control.

Any criteria used should preferably be measurable in quantifiable terms. The best criteria are financial ones.

The scheme should be sensitive enough to ensure that rewards are proportionate to achievements.

The individual should be able to calculate the reward he would receive for a given level of achievement.

The scheme should be acceptable to and benefit the company as well as the participants.

The scheme should operate in conjunction with a sound salary structure in which individuals are paid according to the level of responsibility carried in their job.

The scheme should be easy to administer and to understand and it should be tailored to meet the requirements of the company operating it.

Constraints should be built into the scheme which ensure that staff cannot receive inflated bonuses which may not be directly related to their own efforts.

The formula for calculating the bonus and the conditions under which it is paid should be clearly defined.

The scheme should contain provisions for a regular review, say every two or three years, which could result in the scheme being changed or discontinued.

Bonus Schemes for Senior Executives:

Incentive bonus schemes vary widely in complexity, size of bonus paid and the number and level of staff covered.

The majority of schemes in operation in the United Kingdom use some measure of company profitability to determine bonus although additional criteria are sometimes incorporated in the scheme.

The main types of schemes are:
bonus fund scheme

individual bonus scheme related to company profitability

individual bonus scheme related to an individual target

6.10 SHARE OWNERSHIP SCHEMES

The main advantages:

> they provide participants with a stake in the company which should increase their commitment to its interests
>
> the reward is related to growth in company profitability and its status in the market
>
> an increase in share price benefits both the participating employees and the shareholders
>
> they are potentially a useful device in high risk situations, especially when directors or executives are involved in new ventures or in turning round loss situations
>
> possible taxation advantages which may exist from time to time

The main disadvantages:

> the actual size of the gain may be difficult to forecast
>
> staff are generally unable to relate the size of the reward to their own performance
>
> the size of the reward may be subject to stock market fluctuations which are not connected with the performance of the company
>
> the rewards will not be received for a number of years
>
> it is not possible to predict accurately the tax situation when shares are encashed
>
> the scheme needs to be approved by shareholders in General Meeting;
>
> institutional investors have set ownership guidelines for share schemes
>
> if restricted to executives, they are socially divisive and increase the 'we/they' attitudes — the Government savings-related scheme introduced in 1973 was an attempt to overcome this problem
>
> there is no proof that these schemes do increase identification and commitments

Comparison with the advantages of Bonus Schemes:

> bonus schemes may be more easily designed to relate both to company profitability and to individual performance
>
> it is normally easy to calculate the reward received for a given level of performance
>
> approval is not required from the shareholders
>
> the tax situation is relatively straightforward
>
> the company retains greater control of the rewards given to individual staff
>
> a bonus scheme can be discontinued at any time and limits can be imposed which restrict the maximum bonus payable

Management Development

Is there any evidence that:

the organisation is finding it difficult to provide for management succession, i.e. to fill from within management vacancies arising from expansion, promotion, retirement, death or wastage?

the performance of individual managers or groups of managers needs to be improved in general or in particular areas?

Are records maintained of:

the future needs of the organisation for managers?

the names of individuals who have potential for promotion?

Have any formal plans been made to provide for management succession and to improve the performance of existing managers by:

counselling individual managers and preparing career development and training plans for them?

training programmes using internal and/or external courses?

job rotation?

Manpower Planning

In general is needed when:

a new section, department or site is to be opened, closed or re-organised
an organisation expands or contracts

sections of staff or other workforce approach retirement

jobs are re-designed through introduction of new technology of production methods or their expected development reliance is placed on specialist employees in a scarce labour market or recruitment generally

promotion and career planning is necessary for greater job satisfaction and motivation

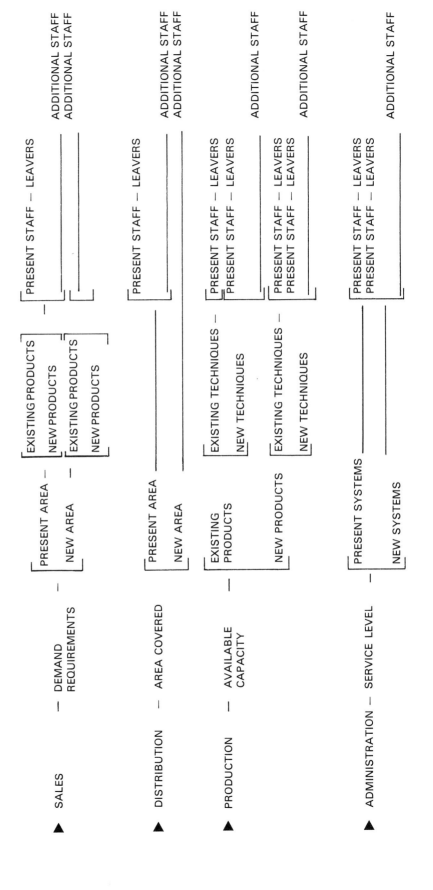

6.12 ELEMENTS OF A MANPOWER PLAN

MANPOWER REQUIREMENTS
REPLACEMENT RECRUITMENT

▲ SALES — DEMAND REQUIREMENTS

PRESENT AREA —
- EXISTING PRODUCTS
  - PRESENT STAFF — LEAVERS
    - ADDITIONAL STAFF
    - ADDITIONAL STAFF
- NEW PRODUCTS

NEW AREA —
- EXISTING PRODUCTS
- NEW PRODUCTS

▲ DISTRIBUTION — AREA COVERED

PRESENT AREA
- PRESENT STAFF — LEAVERS
  - ADDITIONAL STAFF
  - ADDITIONAL STAFF

NEW AREA

▲ PRODUCTION — AVAILABLE CAPACITY

EXISTING PRODUCTS
- EXISTING TECHNIQUES —
  - PRESENT STAFF — LEAVERS
- NEW TECHNIQUES
  - PRESENT STAFF — LEAVERS
    - ADDITIONAL STAFF

NEW PRODUCTS
- EXISTING TECHNIQUES —
  - PRESENT STAFF — LEAVERS
  - PRESENT STAFF — LEAVERS
- NEW TECHNIQUES
  - ADDITIONAL STAFF

▲ ADMINISTRATION — SERVICE LEVEL

PRESENT SYSTEMS
- PRESENT STAFF — LEAVERS
- PRESENT STAFF — LEAVERS

NEW SYSTEMS
- ADDITIONAL STAFF

6.13 MANPOWER PLANNING

Are adequate manpower records maintained which show:

> the numbers employed in each main occupational category?
> the age distribution of employees?
> the turnover of employees analysed by occupation and reason for leaving?

Are forecasts made of future manpower requirements in terms of numbers and skills for each of the main occupational groups?

Are the forecasts based on reliable data concerning:

> factors affecting the demand for manpower, for example:
>> expansions or contractions in activities carried out by the organisation as shown in corporate plans
>> future changes in technology or methods of working
> factors affecting the supply of manpower, for example
>> promotions
>> retirements
>> wastage from within the organisation
>> the availability of suitable manpower from outside

Are functional and/or departmental forecasts of manpower requirements obtained on a regular basis and collated to form an overall manpower plan?

Are manpower forecasts translated into realistic plans for satisfying requirements by:

> recruitment
> re-deployment
> training or re-training
> improving the utilisation or improving the productivity of employees

6.14 RECRUITMENT AND SELECTION WITHIN A MANPOWER PLAN

Are recruitment programmes based on manpower plans?

Is any attempt made to reduce the number of employees to be recruited from external sources by:

> introducing measures to reduce labour turnover?
> improving the utilisation and productivity of employees?
> training or re-training employees?
> promoting or transferring employees?

Are standardised procedures laid down for:
> submitting and approving requisitions for staff?
> advertising?
> obtaining references?

Are standard job descriptions and man specifications available for each of the main categories of employees who are recruited regularly?

Have the personnel staff and the managers responsible for interviewing applicants been trained in interviewing techniques?

Are selection tests used?
If so, have they been properly evaluated to ensure that they are both valid and reliable?

Do interviewers conduct a properly structured interview based on job descriptions and man specifications and using defined criteria for assessing candidates?

Is there any evidence that there are undue delays in completing the recruitment procedures and filling vacancies?
If so, why?

Are there any problems in recruiting the number or quality of employees required?
If so, why?

Are all possible sources of recruits explored thoroughly, for example,
    universities
    technical colleges
    schools
    the services
    employment exchanges
    agencies
    friends
    relations of employees
    ex-employees

Are any other methods of attracting applicants used, for example:
    direct mail
    exhibitions
    tours of the company
    visits to universities
    schools

Is enough effort being made to produce a favourable image of the organisation as a place in which to work by maintaining contact with universities, schools and employment agencies, by press publicity and by the use of recruitment literature?

Are induction programmes in use which give new employees adequate information about:
    terms and conditions of employment
    history of company
    structure of organisation
    products produced with brief descriptions
    introduction to senior management

6.15 TRAINING WITHIN A MANPOWER PLAN

Has the organisation clearly defined training policies covering:
    the objectives of training?
    the scope of the training schemes?
    the limitations of expenditure on training?
    have these the commitment of management?

Are training needs assessed on the basis of:
    manpower forecasts?
    job analysis?
    performance reviews?

Are training plans prepared setting out:
    problem areas?
    proposed action?
    responsibility for action?
    costs of the proposals?
    future benefits?

Are the training needs of each of the main categories of employees adequately catered for by the training plan and the existing training schemes? Are these flexible?

With regard to internal training programmes and courses:
    are these based on a proper assessment of collective and individual training needs?

    are the overall objectives of courses clearly defined, if possible in terms of standards of performance to be attained?

    is the syllabus logically planned and properly related to the overall objectives?

    are the individuals responsible for the training properly trained — and effective in conducting the courses?

    do the programmes consist of a balanced mix of formal instruction, discussion, projects, case studies and practice as appropriate?

    are adequate steps taken to follow-up after training to ensure that what has been taught is effectively being put into practice?

are training programmes evaluated and modified in the light of the follow-up action?

Are external courses selected carefully on the basis of assessments of:
individual training needs?
the relevance and value of the course in relation to the training needs?

Is follow-up action taken to assess the value of the course to the individual and the organisation?

Can external consultants/speakers be used within the internal training programme?

What involvement is there with the Government Training Board?

Are there any committees within the industry service that can offer advice on training matters?

Can tailored individual external courses be used to supplement internal and ordinary external training?

Do:

regard him as a challenge to existing management skills
set him clear objectives and aggressive deadlines
make time to discuss his ideas and suggestions
challenge his ideas and be constructively critical
treat him as a valued member of his team
be quick to praise him for outstanding achievement
see that his salary increases reflect his extra contribution
ask for his suggestions and ideas on some of the existing problems
nominate him for courses which would assist his development
request only those reports which are required

Do not:

allow him to be viewed as a threat to other peoples security
leave him to guess what he is expected to achieve
always be 'too busy' to see him
display indifference or be negative and carping
make him constantly aware of senior status
ignore his achievements (or allow his credits to be stolen)
reward him exactly the same as everyone else
be excessively secretive or discourage his interest
deny him opportunities in case he should appear more knowledgeable than you
keep badgering for reports which you promptly file

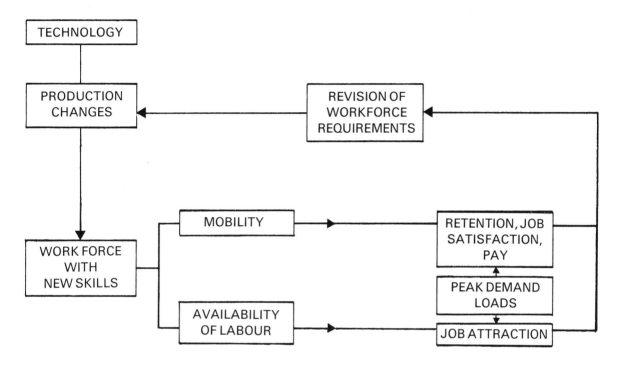

What attracts employees away from an organisation?:

> high earnings
> furthering one's career
> alternative job opportunities

What pushes employees out of an organisation?:

> need to avoid personal conflicts
> running down of staff
> induction crisis
> pressures from shortage of labour
> pressures from changed working requirements or conditions

Reasons for discharge

> unsuitable
> disciplinary reasons
> redundancy
> shortage of materials
> seasonal fluctuation
> restricted operations

Reasons for resignation:

> remuneration
> hours of work
> physical working conditions
> dissatisfaction with job
> relationship with:
>> fellow workers
>> supervisors
> personal betterment
> national service
> transport difficulties
> housing difficulties
> domestic responsibilities
> illness or accident
> marriage
> pregnancy
> move from district
> retirement
> death

Organisation requirements:

> the job title of the individual to whom the job holder reports
> the job titles of each of the individuals reporting directly to the job holder
> a summary for each immediate subordinate of the overall purpose of the job and the main functions or activities which are carried out or for which responsibility attaches
> wherever possible quantitative data should be obtained on the scale of the activities of each subordinate or the section controlled by the subordinate
> details of the organisation structure under each subordinate, including the number and types of staff they supervise.
> (It is often only necessary to go down to the level immediately below the subordinate although there may be occasions when a fuller picture of the organisation structure is required.)

Questions designed to assess the relative importance of tasks:

> what would you regard as your most important duties?
> what are the duties which take up a significant proportion of your time?
> which aspect of the job causes you most problems?
> how in broad terms, do you find your time is being spent in a typical day, week or month?
> how much time do you find you are spending:
>> in meetings with two or more people
>> in face-to-face discussions with your superior, subordinates, or colleagues with other contacts outside the company
>> writing reports or memoranda
>> thinking about plans, policies or problems

Accountability

Employees understanding:

are you expected to formulate your own targets or are these given to you?

how much freedom have you to act within a given policy?

who approves your operating plans and budgets?

how far can you go in changing the organisation structure of your department or re-allocating duties without reference to your superior?

on staffing matters to what extent and to what level can you:

> increase your establishment
> engage staff
> promote staff
> fix salaries on recruitment, transfer or promotion
> re-grade jobs
> award merit increments
> discipline staff
> dismiss staff

with regard to each area of responsibility, on what matters and how often do you approach higher authority (your immediate superior or any other functional head or a committee) in order to:

> make recommendations on a course of action
> obtain approval for a proposed course of action
> seek advice on a problem
> give information on an action you have taken

with regard to each area of responsibility, who makes the final decision on what is to be done?

who decides what control information you produce?

who sees the control information and how is it dealt with?

what is your authority to spend?

Resources controlled by the job:

Obtain details of any resources controlled:

> total number of staff controlled
> annual expenditure budget (broken-down under main headings)
> details of capital expenditure
> value of assets controlled
> size and number of assets controlled, for example, floor space and locations of buildings
> volumes: throughput, items or queries processed, cases dealt with
> turnover
> profit or contribution

Find out for each of the resources controlled its size in proportion to the total resources of the organisation.

Knowledge and skills:

Information must be available on:

> any professional, technical or academic qualifications that are essential or desirable to the effective performance of the job
> the type and amount of experience required — essential or desirable
> the extent to which the job holder has to have knowledge of the procedures and systems used in the organisation

Skills required must be assessed in terms of:

> man management
> administration
> commercial activities
> contacts with other people — to inform, influence, advise or persuade
> communications — written or spoken
> the analytical requirements of the work

Decisions required by job holder:

Establish the level of decision taking involved in the job by analysing:

> the amount of authority the job holder has to take decisions
> the importance of the decisions — this can

be assessed in a number of ways, for example:

the extent to which the job holder personally influences the output, turn-over, profits or contribution for which he is responsible

the amount of influence exerted by the job holder on objectives and targets, corporate or functional policies, short and long range plans

the importance of the objectives, policies and plans with regard to their short and long term impact on the results achieved by the organisation, and their scope in terms of the extent to which they cover the whole or parts of the organisation

the time scale over which decisions are made — this covers the length of time over which plans or programmes are devised and the time span between taking the decision and obtaining the control information which will indicate its effectiveness

Difficulty of the decisions

This can be assessed by checking with regard to each area of decision:

the amount of guidance received from superiors

the existence of clearly defined procedures or precedents and the extent to which the job holder has to use judgment in using the procedures or applying the precedents

any problems in obtaining the information required to take the decisions

any problems in forecasting the outcome of decisions

the amount of original thinking or creativity required to solve problems

Job complexity:

The complexity of the job should be assessed by obtaining information on:

the number or range of different functions or activities controlled — a lead on this should be provided by an analysis of the extent to which the jobs of immediate subordinates vary in responsibility or the activities they carry out

the number of units controlled and the differences between them

the range and variety of products which the job holder produces, markets, sells or distributes

the range and variety of equipment for which the job holder is responsible or which he uses himself

the range and variety of contacts made by the job holder inside and outside the organization

the variety of skills used by the job holder

6.21 JOB EVALUATION/ PERFORMANCE ASSESSMENT

The main types of performance assessment are:

- overall assessment
- guideline assessment
- grading
- merit rating
- critical incident
- target setting

Performance appraisal:

If there exists a systematic performance appraisal procedure, has the method any of the following weaknesses where:

- managers assess undefined personality traits rather than comparing actual performance against agreed standards and targets
- employees are unaware of the results of the performance review except as it affects their salary increments
- managers do not attempt to hold counselling meetings with their staff to discuss strengths and weaknesses and agree training and development needs
- performance review reports are not used to identify training and development needs or to establish potential for promotion
- the system is over-elaborate

Assessing Potential:

- has the employee been long enough in his present job to form an assessment?
- what are the employee's views about the present job?
- in the light of the answers to the above questions, how long should the employee continue in the present job?
- what sort of things can the employee do well?
- what sort of things is the employee less good at?
- what are the employee's interests and ambitions?
- what jobs could the employee move to, in the short and longer term?
- what further training and experience does the employee require before promotion?
- can the employee get the training and experience required in the present job or have special arrangements to be made?

6.22 CHOICE OF JOB EVALUATION SCHEME

The choice of approach will depend on a number of considerations, the main ones being:

- the size and complexity of the organisation
- the type of jobs to be covered
- the type of organisation and its management style
- the climate of industrial and employee relations
- equal pay
- cost
- time and resources available
- the general pay situation

Methods used to determine salary levels, e.g.:

- no formal method
- job evaluation

If no formal method is used, what influences decisions on salary levels:

- nationally negotiated salary changes
- movements in the cost of living
- movements in market rates
- pressures from staff unions
- pressures from increases in hourly paid workers' rates or earnings

If a system of job evaluation is used:

- is it non-analytical (e.g. whole job ranking) or analytical (e.g. factor comparison)?
- if non-analytical:
  - is ranking based on detailed job descriptions and comparisons with bench mark jobs?
  - are paired comparisons used to rank jobs?
- if analytical:
  - do the factors represent significant criteria for comparing the jobs?
  - do the factors overlap?
- is the system understood and accepted by employees?
- is the system cost-effective in the sense that it is simple to maintain and not over-elaborate in relation to the accuracy of the results achieved?

have the staff administering the system been properly trained in its use?

are regular surveys carried out to compare market rates?

has the organisation a policy on where its salary and wage levels should be in relation to market rates?

how do salary and wage levels compare with market rates — locally and nationally?

how do fringe benefits compare with those provided elsewhere?

are individuals progressed through job grades and promoted on the basis of formal assessments of performance and potential?

Which way was the scheme introduced?

was it specially developed within the organisation?

was it a proprietary brand introduced with the help of consultants?

was it a scheme taken from the shelf without any attempt being made to adapt it to the needs of the organisation?

Schemes developed or introduced with the help of consultants:

check on the use of bench-mark jobs:
was the sample large enough?
was the samply fully representative?
did the sample include jobs which would facilitate both internal and external comparisons?

check on the methods used to analyse jobs:
was the analysis confined to existing job descriptions? — if so, how adequate were they for this purpose?
were job holders required to complete questionnaires and how effectively were they completed?
were job holders interviewed — if so, were check lists used which ensured that all points were covered, and was the information obtained from job holders confirmed by the superiors?

check on the job descriptions:
are they clearly divided into sections covering the overall purpose of the job, the organisational relationships of the job holder, the main activities carried out, and an analysis, where applicable, of the job in terms of the factors used in evaluation scheme?

does the description of the overall purpose of the job clearly convey in one or two sentences the main function or role of the job holder in a way which distinguishes the job from others?

does the description identify the job title of the individual to whom the job holder is responsible and the job titles of all the individuals directly responsible to him?

are the separate activities clearly defined?

does the description of each activity convey adequately what is done without the use of unnecessary verbiage or vague adjectives?

are quantitative examples given where relevant?

does the job description adequately convey the level of authority exercised by the job holder, the amount of direction and guidance received from line or functional superiors, the relationships maintained within and outside the organisation, the complexity of the job and the knowledge and skills that are required to do it?

are the resources controlled by the job holder adequately defined?

check on the competence of those who developed the scheme:
what was their prior experience?
what training have they received?

Job ranking, as a means to evaluation:
were rank orders established by paired comparisons?
was a team of trained judges used to rank the jobs?
how were the jobs slotted into grades?

A job classification type scheme:
were the grades defined on the basis of a job analysis and job ranking exercise?
is the hierarchy of levels of responsibility clearly defined by the descriptions so that successive levels can easily be distinguished from one another?
are the broad grade definitions supplemented by cross references to examples drawn from bench-mark jobs?
how helpful are the grade definitions in

deciding on the grading of jobs in border line cases?

A points type scheme:

are there so many factors that the scheme appears to be unnecessarily complicated?

are the factors appropriate for the jobs covered by the scheme and do they cover the key areas common to all jobs without too much overlap?

are the factors and the levels within the factors adequately defined?

was the weighting of the factors decided on an arbitrary basis or was a special exercise such as multiple regression analysis used to calculate weightings?

could an equally acceptable result be obtained by using a simpler approach such as job classification, supported by market surveys?

were staff given adequate information about the scheme during its development and have they been kept informed subsequently?

Basic features:

entry age for membership
contributions
pension on retirement
cash options on retirement
late retirement
post-retirement pension increases
widows/widowers benefits
early retirement
early leavers
'top hat' arrangements
integration with state provisions
funding

Present arrangements:

The following information should be obtained about the existing pension scheme or schemes:

whether the scheme is self-administered or insured (and in the latter case the annual renewal date)

the total membership of the scheme or schemes

the total scheme salary roll or a list of individual scheme salaries

numbers not included in the schemes and the reasons why

eligibility for membership of the scheme or schemes (is it compulsory?)

entry requirements — minimum and maximum age on entry for men and women

whether the scheme(s) is contributory or non-contributory, and if contributory the scale of contributions

the retirement ages for males and females

the retirement formula and scale of benefits on retirement: for example:

final salary (salary service) — the pension fraction (n/60ths etc.), number years that can count as pensionable service and basis for determining final salary (e.g. average of last three years' salary):

total earnings (average salary) — the ratio of pension to the mean scheme salary in each class (1 per cent or 1½ per cent etc.) and the relationship between pensionable earnings and actual earnings; flat rate or money purchase;

lump sum option (commutation rights) — availability of option, the amount that can be obtained and the basis for calculating the amount

late retirement — the provisions for improving the pension if the employee works on after normal retiring date and the formula used, if any, to determine the improvement

pension increases — the provisions, if any, for relating increases to a cost of living index or a pre-determined percentage figure, such as 3 per cent compound a year

widows' pensions and lump sum provisions after death in service

widows' pensions after death in retirement — whether commencing immediately on death or following a guaranteed period of payment of the member's pension

early retirement pension provisions

early leavers — arrangements for:
> returning contributions
> freezing rights to accrued benefit
> transferring accrued benefits to new employer

top hat scheme — provisions for providing individuals with a greater pension benefit than that given by the main fund

salary sacrifice — provisions for allowing staff to sacrifice part of their salary to gain an enhanced pension (maximum benefits are however related to the reduced salary)

the basis upon which pensionable earnings calculated — are bonuses, commission, overtime or other emoluments included and if so, is an average of previous years, usually three, taken

integration — whether or not the scheme is integrated (i.e. takes account of the State flat rate pension) and if it is, the method of integration, for example:
> full integration
> 'salary disregard'
> lower fraction throughout
> variable fractions

6.24 CHANGING A PENSION SCHEME

The steps to take when introducing or amending a pension scheme are as follows:

> analyse present arrangements
>
> make a preliminary assessment of the need to change present arrangements and select advisers to help in developing the new or revised scheme
>
> > identify and evaluate the alternative arrangements for each aspect of the pension scheme from the point of view of
> >
> > > the requirements of the Revenue code of approval
> > >
> > > latest legislation
> > >
> > > costs
> > >
> > > funding and administration
>
> consider in the light of the information obtained from the analysis above the case for making the scheme contributory or non-contributory and the level of contributions required
>
> consult staff
>
> make a preliminary decision on:
>
> > the range and level of benefits that should be provided
> >
> > contribution arrangements
> >
> > funding and administrative arrangements
>
> prepare a clear and easy to read summary of the proposed arrangements for discussion with staff
>
> make any final modifications to the scheme in the light of the views of the staff
>
> issue a provisional notification of the scheme to staff
>
> obtain approval from the Inland Revenue
>
> complete all administrative arrangements with the trustees and, where appropriate, the insurance company
>
> ensure that a concise, informative and readable booklet is prepared for the staff
>
> communicate details of the new scheme to staff — be prepared to allow time for discussions with individual members of staff on how the scheme affects them

See Also

7 Finance and Accounting

7.1 SOURCES OF FINANCE

Short-term:
Up to one year
      bank overdrafts
      bill financing
      suppliers credit
      invoice discounting
      credit factoring

Medium-term:
One to five years
      hire purchase
      deferred instalment
      equipment leasing
      term loans

Long-term:
Over five years
      long-term loans
      investors — ordinary shares
                — preference shares
      debenture or similar loan stock

7.2 BALANCE SHEET STRUCTURE

A Balance Sheet is a summary of   ASSETS and LIABILITIES

ASSETS are generally classified into . . . .   FIXED ASSETS and CURRENT ASSETS

FIXED ASSETS consist of . . . .   TANGIBLE ASSETS Property
                                        Plant & Machinery
                                        Motor Vehicles

     INTANGIBLE ASSETS Goodwill
                                     Patents

FIXED ASSETS can be valued at . . . .   Cost
     Cost less depreciation
     Valuation
     Replacement Value
     (or a combination of each)

CURRENT ASSETS can be valued at . . . .   Realisable amount (e.g. expectation of amount receivable from debtors after reserving for possible bad debts)
     Cost, including an amount for the value of work in progress (i.e. in the case of stock)

LIABILITIES are stated at . . . .   The monetary amount necessary to discharge the indebtedness.

It is essential when a balance sheet is used as the basis of calculations for:-
    Net Worth or Net Value
    Return on Capital
    Fixed v Current Investment
    Ratio comparison
    Borrowings
    Insurance

that the method used to arrive at asset values is identified

FIXED ASSETS should be financed by Permanent or Long-Term sources of Capital
CURRENT ASSETS should be financed by Short Term sources of Capital

Stylised Balance Sheet in 7.3 shows this by example

7.3 BALANCE SHEET CLASSIFICATION

USES OF FINANCE

FIXED ASSETS

Goodwill
Land & buildings
Plant & machinery
Vehicles

Trade investments
Associated company
investments

CURRENT ASSETS

Cash & marketable
securities

OTHER ASSETS

Stocks
Debtors

Fixed assets

Working assets

Permanent Investment

Circulating Investment

Total capital = Total assets

SOURCE OF FINANCE

SHAREHOLDER'S (OWNERS)

Ordinary shares
Reserves

LENDERS' INVESTMENT
(LONG TERM)

Preference shares
Debentures
Long term loans
Deferred tax

CURRENT LIABILITIES

Overdraft
Creditors

Long term sources

Short term sources

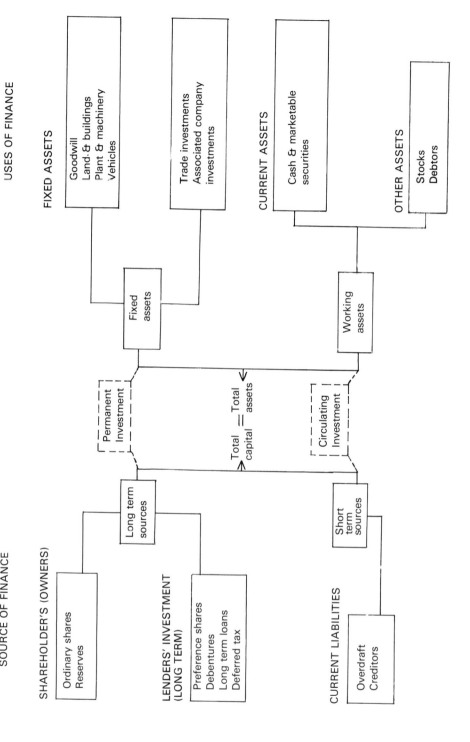

FIXED ASSETS	—Property investment	Ascertain Cost and/or Valuation amounts (Source: Balance Sheet, Notes to Balance Sheet and Directors Report as shown in the annual accounts)
		Age of freehold properties or leasehold properties.
		Date of Valuation
		Basis of Valuation
		Realisable Value
		Alternative investment, e.g. sale and lease back
		Policy relating to depreciation, rate of write-off by classification of type of building or structure
		Value of unexpired lease
	— Plant, Machinery and Vehicles:	Type of plant, location. Value to business
		Depreciation policy and adequacy in inflationary periods
		Obsolescence of processes, changes in technology
		Replacement cost and availability of alternative equipment
	— Goodwill:	Is value justified and does it represent value of **super profits? (the profits in excess of an acheivable return for the type of business)**
		What is the write-off policy?
CURRENT ASSETS	— Stock and work in Progress:	What indication is given regarding basis of value e.g. inclusion of overheads?
		How consistent is the valuation policy?
		Is the industry in a fast moving consumer sector — rate of depreciation of product lines
	— Debtors:	Adequacy of provision for bad debts
		Length of credit given and currency in which receivable.

CONTINGENT
LIABILITIES

Determine the basis of valuation in hire purchase transactions and Long-Term contracts. Also amount of contingent liabilities which could materialise into actual liability and possible effect on liquidity.

Markets:

    growth of sales
    growth of market share
    length of order book/sales
    debtors/sales

Capital:

    net profit after tax/shareholders' funds
    price/earnings ratio
    interest paid/borrowed capital
    total profit/interest paid
    borrowede capital/equity capital
    earnings per share
    dividend paid/market value
    dividend paid/attributable profit

Suppliers:

    suppliers' prices index
    suppliers' lead time
    days orders overdue
    creditors/purchases
    cash, debtors, marketable securities/current liabilities
    value of goods returned or credited/ purchases

Employees:

    number of leavers/average numbers employed
    average age of senior staff: now/five years ago
    'output' per employee

Assets:

    net profit before tax to total assets
    net profit before tax to net assets
    current assets/current liabilities
    liquid assets/current liabilities
    actual output/maximum output

Ratios	Capital base	Profit base
1 Return on Total Assets	Total Assets	Net Profit before all interest charges and taxation
2 Return on Total Tangible Assets	Total Assets but excluding intangibles e.g. Goodwill, Patents etc.	As for ratio (1)
3 Return on Total Operating Assets	Total Assets but excluding intangibles and investments	As for ratio (1) but excluding investment income
4 Return on Net Assets	Total Assets less current liabilities	As for ratio (3)
5 Return on Net Tangible Assets	Total tangible assets less current liabilities	As for ratio (1)
6 Return on Net Operating Assets	Total operating assets less current liabilities	As for ratio (3)
7 Return on Long Term Capital Employed	Capital + Reserves (Total or net of intangibles) + Deferred Tax + Borrowing (Total or long term only) + Minority interests	Net profit before and after taxation
8 Return on Shareholders' funds	Capital + Reserves (Intangibles must be included)	Net profit after charging all interest and taxation and adjusting for minority interests
9 Return to holders of Ordinary shares	Issued Ordinary Capital + Reserves	As for ratio (8) but after Preference Dividends
10 Earnings Yield (at par value of shares)	Issued Ordinary Capital	As for ratio (9)
11 Earnings per share	Number of Ordinary shares in issue	As for ratio (9)

7.7 RETURN ON CAPITAL RATIOS

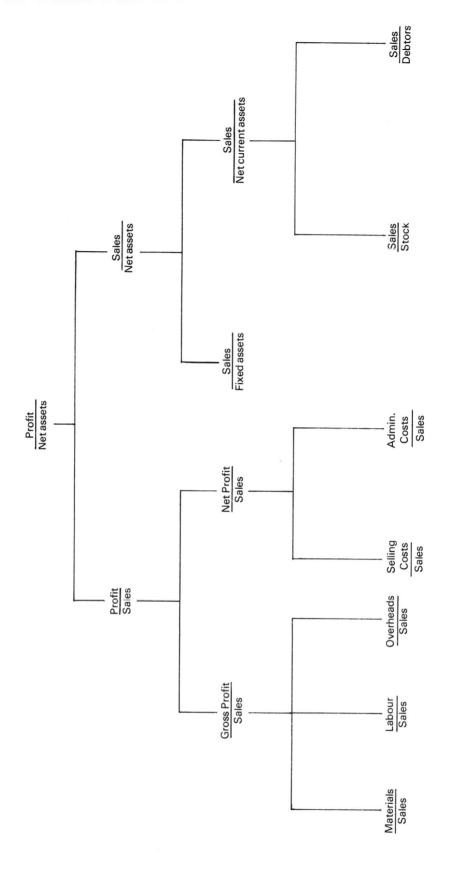

All ratios to be stated in percentages

7.8 GEARING, CASH AND WORKING CAPITAL RATIOS

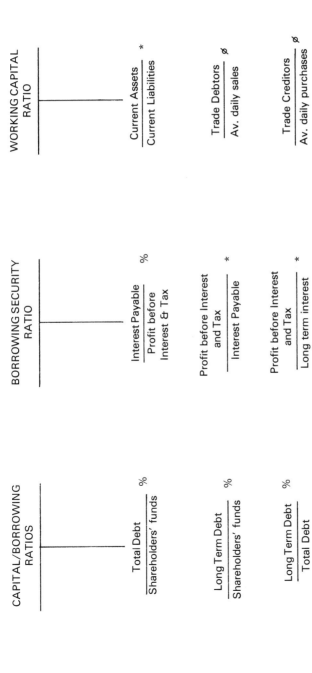

CAPITAL/BORROWING RATIOS

$$\frac{\text{Total Debt}}{\text{Shareholders' funds}} \%$$

$$\frac{\text{Long Term Debt}}{\text{Shareholders' funds}} \%$$

$$\frac{\text{Long Term Debt}}{\text{Total Debt}} \%$$

$$\frac{\text{Total Debt}}{\text{Total Assets}} \%$$

BORROWING SECURITY RATIO

$$\frac{\text{Interest Payable}}{\text{Profit before Interest \& Tax}} \%$$

$$\frac{\text{Profit before Interest and Tax}}{\text{Interest Payable}} *$$

$$\frac{\text{Profit before Interest and Tax}}{\text{Long term interest}} *$$

WORKING CAPITAL RATIO

$$\frac{\text{Current Assets}}{\text{Current Liabilities}} *$$

$$\frac{\text{Trade Debtors}}{\text{Av. daily sales}} \emptyset$$

$$\frac{\text{Trade Creditors}}{\text{Av. daily purchases}} \emptyset$$

$$\frac{\text{Stock}}{\text{Av. daily raw material cost of sales}} \emptyset$$

LIQUIDITY RATIO

$$\frac{\text{Cash + Investment}}{\text{Trade Creditors}} \%$$

$$\frac{\text{Cash, Debtors and Investments}}{\text{Total current liabilities}} \%$$

* number of times

$\emptyset$ number of days

7.10 MANUFACTURING RATIOS

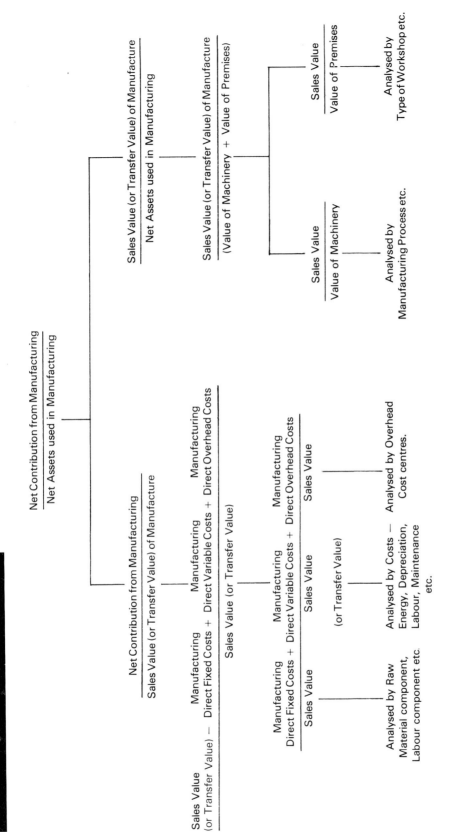

$$\frac{\text{Net Contribution from Manufacturing}}{\text{Net Assets used in Manufacturing}}$$

$$\frac{\text{Net Contribution from Manufacturing}}{\text{Sales Value (or Transfer Value) of Manufacture}}$$

$$\frac{\text{Manufacturing}}{\text{Sales Value (or Transfer Value)}}$$

Sales Value (or Transfer Value) − Direct Fixed Costs + Direct Variable Costs + Direct Overhead Costs

$$\frac{\text{Manufacturing}}{\text{Sales Value}} \quad \text{Direct Fixed Costs + Direct Variable Costs + Direct Overhead Costs}$$

$$\frac{\text{Manufacturing Direct Fixed Costs}}{\text{Sales Value}}$$

(or Transfer Value)

$$\frac{\text{Direct Variable Costs}}{\text{Sales Value}}$$

$$\frac{\text{Direct Overhead Costs}}{\text{Sales Value}}$$

Analysed by Raw Material component, Labour component etc.

Analysed by Costs — Energy, Depreciation, Labour, Maintenance etc.

Analysed by Overhead Cost centres.

$$\frac{\text{Sales Value (or Transfer Value) of Manufacture}}{\text{Net Assets used in Manufacturing}}$$

$$\frac{\text{Sales Value (or Transfer Value) of Manufacture}}{\text{(Value of Machinery + Value of Premises)}}$$

$$\frac{\text{Sales Value}}{\text{Value of Machinery}}$$

$$\frac{\text{Sales Value}}{\text{Value of Premises}}$$

Analysed by Manufacturing Process etc.

Analysed by Type of Workshop etc.

All rates to be stated in percentages

7.11 MACHINE CAPACITY RATIOS

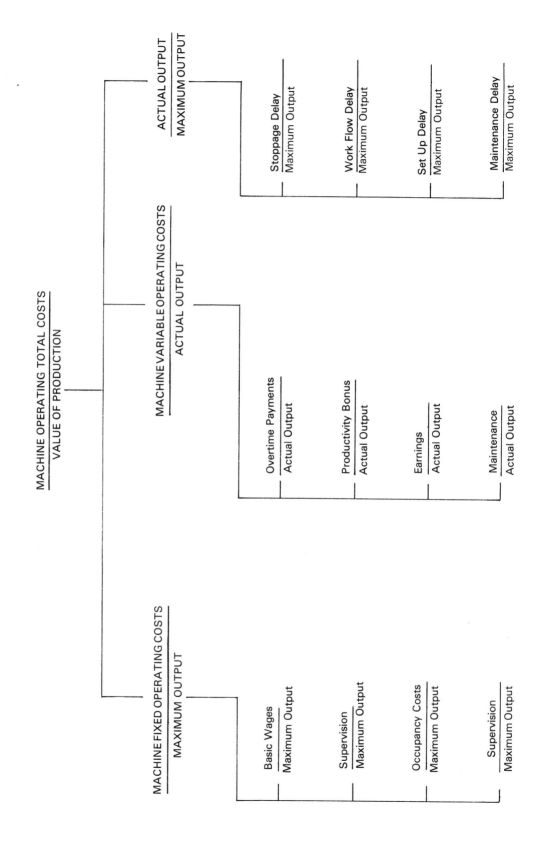

$$\frac{\text{MACHINE OPERATING TOTAL COSTS}}{\text{VALUE OF PRODUCTION}}$$

$$\frac{\text{MACHINE FIXED OPERATING COSTS}}{\text{MAXIMUM OUTPUT}}$$

$$\frac{\text{Basic Wages}}{\text{Maximum Output}}$$

$$\frac{\text{Supervision}}{\text{Maximum Output}}$$

$$\frac{\text{Occupancy Costs}}{\text{Maximum Output}}$$

$$\frac{\text{Supervision}}{\text{Maximum Output}}$$

$$\frac{\text{MACHINE VARIABLE OPERATING COSTS}}{\text{ACTUAL OUTPUT}}$$

$$\frac{\text{Overtime Payments}}{\text{Actual Output}}$$

$$\frac{\text{Productivity Bonus}}{\text{Actual Output}}$$

$$\frac{\text{Earnings}}{\text{Actual Output}}$$

$$\frac{\text{Maintenance}}{\text{Actual Output}}$$

$$\frac{\text{ACTUAL OUTPUT}}{\text{MAXIMUM OUTPUT}}$$

$$\frac{\text{Stoppage Delay}}{\text{Maximum Output}}$$

$$\frac{\text{Work Flow Delay}}{\text{Maximum Output}}$$

$$\frac{\text{Set Up Delay}}{\text{Maximum Output}}$$

$$\frac{\text{Maintenance Delay}}{\text{Maximum Output}}$$

7.12 LABOUR UTILISATION RATIOS

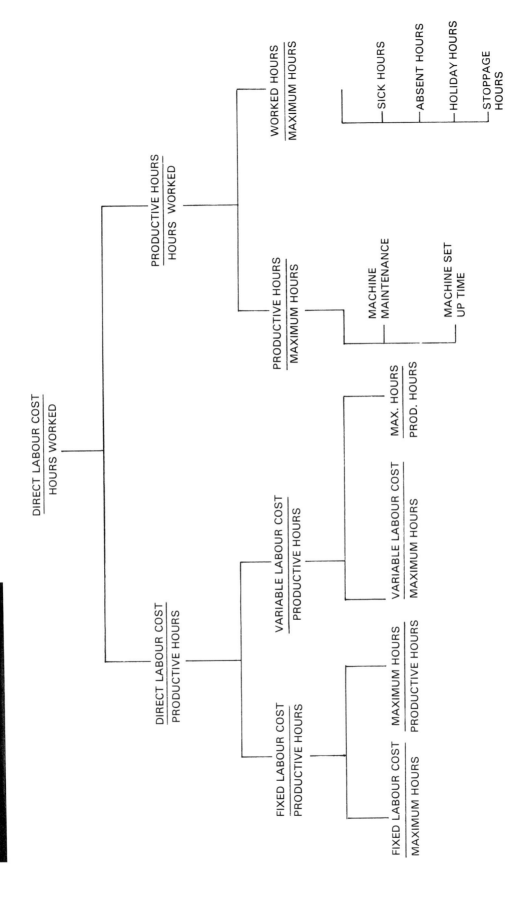

Areas to be considered are the relationship between a company and:

its markets
the providers of its capital, both risk and loan
its suppliers
its employees
its trading
its asset turnover

Market ratios:
competitions return on capital
competitions capital expenditure/sales
competitions/sales
competitions research/sales
competitions market-share/total market

Providers of capital:
return on shareholder's funds
earnings yield
dividend yield

Share price/earnings
shareholder's funds/borrowings

Supplies:
suppliers' return on capital
suppliers' share of market
suppliers' damaged or deficient supplies/purchases

Employees:
efficiency — actual hours worked/actual **production hours available**
activity — actual production hours/budgeted production hours
capacity — actual hours worked/budgeted hours

Trading
gross profit/sales
net profit/sales
stock turnover/cost of sales
materials/cost of production
labour/cost of production

Production:
production overheads/cost of production

Asset turnover:
working capital/sales
debtors/sales
creditors/purchases
fixed assets/sales
fixed assets/working assets

Return on assets:
ratios as for market ratios but relating to company

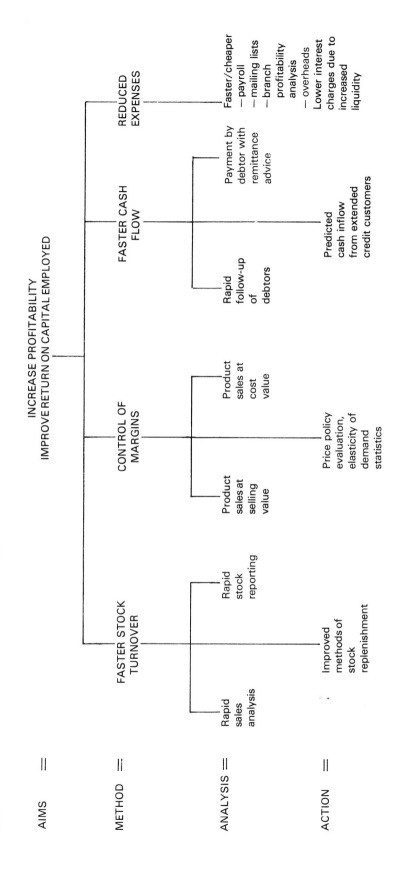

7.14 FINANCIAL OBJECTIVES OF MANAGEMENT IN RATIO TERMS

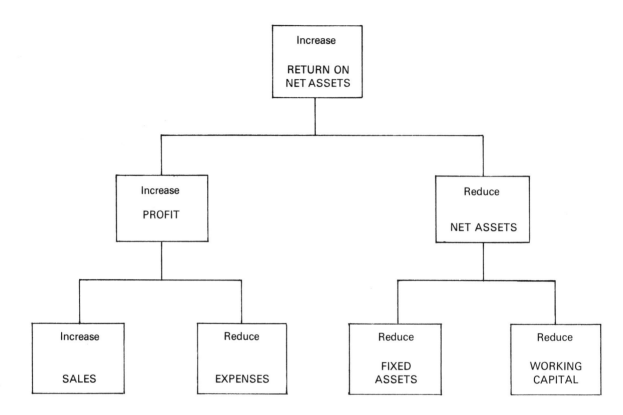

7.16 'INTERFIRM' COMPARISON OF COMPANIES

Problems of comparability:

> how similar are the other firms?
> how can the information be obtained?
> how reliable is the information?

Comparable companies:

> competitors
> potential competitors
> firms operating in fields the company might enter

Sources of comparison:

> company accounts
> trade information
> trade associations
> sales literature

7.17 TYPES OF REPORTS IN MANAGEMENT INFORMATION SYSTEMS

Profitability reports by:

> product
> division
> area
> customer group
> channel of distribution
> organisation
> profit responsibility centre

Cost reports of:

> labour analyses — direct labour
> labour analyses — indirect labour
> productive labour variances
> non-productive labour variances
> direct expense analysis
> productivity analysis — direct labour
> overtime payment analysis
> analysis of spoilt work, rework and scrap
> material analyses
> manufacturing overhead analysis
> administrative cost analysis
> marketing cost analysis (order getting costs)
> distribution cost analysis (order-filling costs)
> product costs
> cost of production
> cost of sales
> cost analyses for every responsibility centre and their constituent cost centres

Sundry reports on:

> orders received
> orders delivered
> overdue deliveries
> backlog of orders at month-end
> material yields
> cash receipts
> physical output
> research and development progress report
> special studies:
>> analysis and interpretation of problems or trends indicated by other regular reports
>> studies directed towards finding cost reduction opportunities

What is management accounting?

it is the interpretation of financial data for the purposes of day to day management control and decision taking

it uses the same data base as for financial accounting

it relates the present to previous plans

it is unaffected by statutory requirements relating to presentation of accounting information

it takes account of the management structure in terms of individual accountability and responsibility

it is the data recording process within the management information system

How does it operate?

budgets form a part of the management information system

actual results are compared with budgets

budgets are updated when necessary in the form of forecasts

What does a Management Accounting system include?

routine accounting statements

to show budget compared with actual profit

balance sheet

cash flow

capital expenditure

volumes manufactured and sold

performance ratios

variance statement

7.19 FRAMEWORK FOR A MANAGEMENT ACCOUNTING SYSTEM

capital
labour
materials
services
knowledge
plans

THE COMPANY

return on investment
consumer satisfaction
goods and services
goal attainment
market share
salary levels

INPUTS   CONVERSION   OUTPUTS
UNIT

The purpose of a management accounting system is:

to show the cost structure of each product and process so that effective control may be exercised

to facilitate product costing, for inventory valuation and income determination purposes

to identify profit or loss by department, process or job — this can aid in determining the output or products that will lead to the most profitable level of operations

to aid in the pricing decision by distinguishing between fixed and variable costs, thereby establishing lowest price levels

to prevent wastage by the use of an efficient system of stores and wages control

to provide cost estimate data on which to base tenders

to secure more efficient operations, and more effective use of resources, by comparison of results with pre-determined standards (variance analysis) or data supplied by similar firms

to permit the establishing of uniform cost accounting systems for inter-firm comparison purposes

to identify and permit acceptable resource allocation
to measure management accountability

to enable Accountability and Responsibility to be measured

**purpose of management accounting
illustrated**

Management accounting relates to the:-

 Management Structure

 Management Information System

 Budget

 Management Accounting System

and to the interlocking

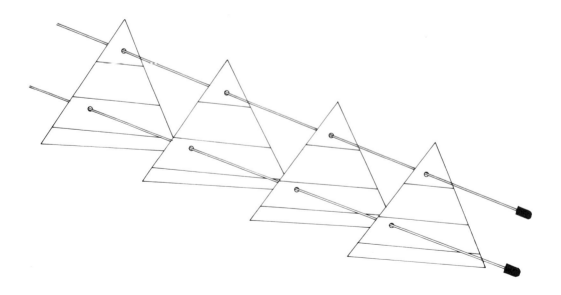

7.20 BUDGETING PRINCIPLES

Budgeting:

is a management tool

is essential for short-term operational planning and control

aims to anticipate change

Budgetary control system conditions depend on the following:

management responsibility must be clear

managers must see their standards and budgets as attainable

the budgetary control information must be understood by those for whom it is designed

training in budgetary control must be effective

the organisation of information production must be appropriate

managers must understand the purposes of the budgetary system

Budgets translate plans into firm parameters in terms of resource generation and utilisation in all areas against which performance can be continually monitored. Budgets can be for any period and cover the main operating areas, e.g.:

profit and loss statements in detail

asset movement
fixed assets including buildings, machinery etc.
stocks and work in progress
debtors
total assets

sales, orders received and orders on hand
manpower
direct and indirect by function
direct and indirect by product
direct and indirect by division

remuneration
direct and indirect by function
budget for standard hours available

stock analysis
by category (e.g. pre-process, work in progress and finished goods)
labour input
material input
write-down and other provisions

expense classification
remuneration
commissions
purchased services
insurance
depreciation

gross margin analysis by products

expense analysis by function and category
production
marketing
engineering

capital expenditure by project
sales analysis by class of customer and product
analysis of floor space
analysis of reserves
balance sheet
cash flow
analysis of research and development projects
manufacturing shop loading and manpower utilisation

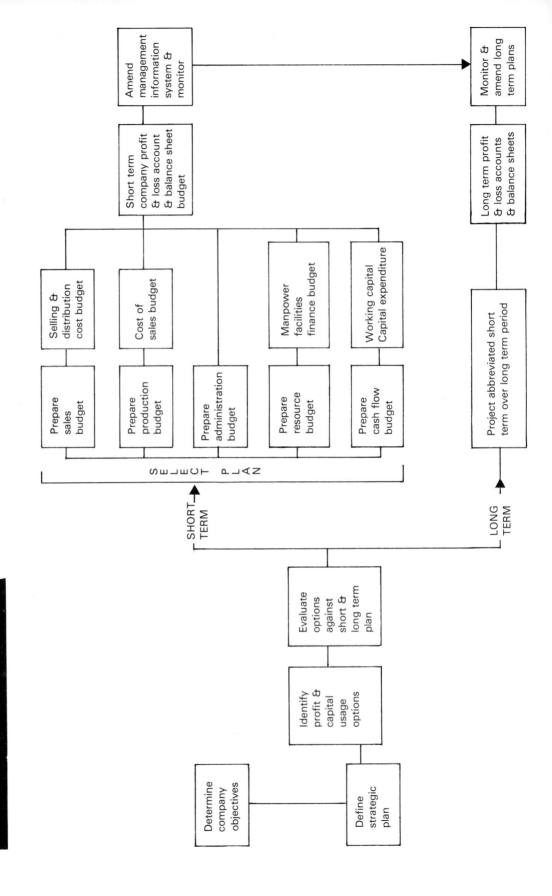

7.21 BUDGETARY CONTROL PROCEDURE

7.22 WEAKNESSES OF BUDGETARY CONTROL

Major problem areas are frequently encountered in the use of budget systems:

they can grow to be so complex, detailed, cumbersome, meaningless and expensive that they become dangerous

budgetary goals may come to supercede organisational goals, requiring care in using budgets as a *means* and not an *end*

budgets tend to hide inefficiencies — provision must be made for re-examination of standards and other bases of planning, by which policies are translated into numerical terms

the use of budgets as punitive or pressure devices defeats their basic purpose

management accountants accept standard rules of thumb without questioning the principles on which they are based and the aims in view

other functional managers have too little understanding of the methods by which costs are calculated and cannot deal with cost allocation arguments

there is a poor reconciliation process with financial accounts

7.23 FORECASTING

Forecasting is an integral part of budgeting
The design of an information system must be based on:

what information should be provided?
in what form should this information be supplied?
to whom should this information be made available?

Actual results should be related to a yardstick of performance — a predetermined plan, budget, or standard. Management information must observe important features of any control system:

accountability
controllability
selectivity

The information used must be:
impartial
valid
reliable
consistent

Good management accounting systems are based upon the following criteria:

the accurate identification of changing costs in products, product groups, markets, key customers, operations and processes

the control of these costs when they are rising, particularly within material usage and in distribution

the provision of information for effective management decisions

A bad management accounting reporting sytem can be detected from these deficiencies:

it does not react to cost inflation quickly enough

a simple costing practice which suited the business when it was small and simple, is no longer sufficient when it is large and complex

a system based upon the extrapolation of historical costs becomes badly distorted during inflation does the budgeting process have top management sponsorship and support?

is the budgeting process seen as being a major tool of management rather than an accounting technique?

can responsible individuals throughout the organisation work to budgets?

is management by objectives (MBO) practised? — if so, do managers meet their objectives and if not, why not?

are the figures in budget compiled on the basis of the same definitions as the actual figures with which they will be compared?

does the budgeting process encourage delegation?

do budgets motivate people in the desired direction?

do all employees — and especially supervisors and managers — fully understand the cost implications of their work and are they able to plan cost expectations accordingly?

do the budget targets lead to objective attainment?

do the budget targets represent reasonably attainable goals?

are budgets flexible in relation to changing conditions?

is the budget used as a tool for co-operative planning and control rather than as an inflexible tool of dominance?

is balance achieved between budgeting for short-run operations and planning long-term strategy?

are plans explicit?

are plans understood?

are plans capable of being adapted to meet change?

who will be affected by future plans and how will these people be affected?

are plans (and objectives) compatible with internal and external constraints?

are plans capable of being monitored (i.e. in quantified format)?

is the company's level of activity expanding or contracting?

what effect does the answer to the preceding question have on:
>   manpower requirements?
>   financial requirements?
>   administrative requirements?

is the time period covered by the budget related to the necessity for, and the possibility of, effective management action?

had consideration been given to adopting rolling budgeting as opposed to purely periodic budgeting?

is the budget built on a thorough knowledge of cost behaviour patterns?

are budgeted expenditures classified in sufficient detail and over sufficient headings to permit the estimating of costs by each major item and function under each area of responsibility?

do budget control reports include reasons as well as results?

is control effort focused on significant devitions from plan only?

are responsible individuals able to help in developing cost targets for themselves and their subordinates?

are tomorrow's winners (i.e. new products) being developed? — if so, have consumer requirements been carefully evaluated?

is consideration being given to the use of new materials, new processes, and new technology?

is the staff function in the budgeting process carefully distinguished from the lone function?

is budgeting part of the duties of the management accountant? — if not, why not and if so, are his terms of reference widely known?

does the company have a budget committee?

are forecasting procedures adequately developed?

is the whole planning/budgeting endeavour based on a careful and continuing evaluation of all major factors (both external and internal) that will affect the future?

is imagination used in identifying other courses of action prior to their evaluation in relation to corporate objectives?

7.25 KEY QUESTIONS FOR EXAMINING ANY ACTIVITY OR EXPENSE

can it be eliminated without much harm to the results?

does it cost more than it is worth?

can it be reduced in scope and cost?

does it do more than is required?

can it be done more cheaply another way?

can it be done more cheaply by someone else?

is there an alternative service from outside which is adequate but cheaper?

can the service or expenses supporting the operation be reduced?

on a management judgement basis, can the operation be sensibly considered to provide its full share of overhead and net profit contribution?

how does it affect other costs in the business?

if you were to start the business again would you include it?

Research and Development	Manufacturing	Marketing	Distribution	Administration
Salaries:	Salaries:	Salaries:	Salaries:	Salaries:
executives	executives	executives	executives	directors
technical	clerical/secretar-	representatives	clerical/secretar-	executives
clerical/secretar-	ial staff	clerical/secretar-	ial staff	clerical/secretarial
ial staff	hourly paid	ial staff	hourly paid	staff
hourly paid	Expenses:	Commission:	Expenses:	temporary staff
Expenses:	travelling	executives	travelling	Expenses:
travelling	motor	representatives	motor	travelling
motor	entertaining	agents	entertaining	motor
entertaining	other	royalties payable	other	entertaining
other	Departmental ex-	Expenses:	Transport:	other
Laboratory:	penses:	travelling	fleet supervision	Office expenses:
services	progress	motor	road fund tax	stationery
consultants' fees	goods inwards	entertaining	insurances	telephone & telex
safety costs	time-keeping	other	painting &	postages
cleaning	tool room	Office expenses:	lettering	mailroom/reception
maintenance	production control	stationery	garage expenses	cleaning
hire of equipment	purchasing	telephone & telex	vehicle running	hire of equipment
consumable items	personnel	postages	costs	maintenance of
sundry materials	drawing office	cleaning	vehicle maintenance	equipment
samples	maintenance	hire of equipment	costs	depreciation of
General:	quality control	maintenance of	vehicle hire charges	equipment
patent cost	General:	equipment	depreciation	EDP expenses:
trademark costs	training costs	depreciation of	Warehousing:	data preparation
(royalties re-	services: e.g.	equipment	rates and rent	operating costs
ceivable)	boilerhouse)	General expenses:	insurances	systems and pro-
subscriptions	waste disposal	training costs	hire of equipment	gramming
training costs	heat, light, power	recruitment	maintenance of	stationery
telephone & telex	insurances	subscriptions	equipment	depreciation of
insurances	rent and rates	hire of premises	depreciation of	equipment
rent and rates	protective cloth-	maintenance	equipment	Financial expenses:
deprecation of	ing	amortization	stocktaking costs	audit fees
equipment	fire & safety	bad debts	Despatch:	bank charges
	equipment	legal expenses	packing and	interest payable
	security	discounts given	packaging	director's fees
	laundering	insurances	sundry materials	superannuation
	cleaning	sales administra-	carriage outwards	secretarial/
	sundry materials	tion	insurances	registrar
	scrap	Promotion expenses:	maintenance of	insurances
	telephone & telex	sales samples	equipment	General Expenses:
	canteen expenses	catalogues/price	depreciation of	training costs
	subscriptions	lists	equipment	heat, light, power
	hire of machinery	advertising agency	General:	subscriptions and
	depreciation of	fees	canteen expenses	donations
	machinery	media costs	telephone & telex	security
		production costs	training costs	personnel and
		PR fees and	heat, light, power	welfare
		expenses		canteen expenses
		Marketing research:		legal and other
		agency fees		charges
		data processing		hire of premises
		charges		rates
		subscriptions		maintenance

TYPE	BASIS OF ALLOCATION
Waiting time	On the one hand, productive man-hours for total productive tasks (whether for sale or for stock); on the other, productive man-hours available from the existing work force after absenteeism and overtime
Work Shop cleaning	If done as a full-time job, probably determined by floor area of factory
Training time	Number of productive workers and rate of labour turnover
Supervision	Number of productive workers
Inspection	When method of inspection has been fixed, number and mix of units produced
Storekeeping and buying	When stock-holding policy has been established, number and mix of units produced
Shop clerical work	Number of productive workers and size of productive workers and size of production batches
Payroll department	Total number of people employed — productive and indirect
Graduated pension contributions	Total gross pay
Power costs	Machine-hours run
Heating and lighting	Floor area or cubic area affected
Rent and rates for premises	In the short run, fixed; in the longer run, determined by total personnel employed, machines installed and required holdings of stock and work in progress — probably rationalised as product volume and mix
Machine lubricants	Machine-hours run
Consumable tools	Production hours, or units produced
Consumable materials	Units produced
Insurance	Valuation of buildings, or stocks or total payroll — dependent on risk insured

Three broad categories:

Blanket Method:
> Where all expenses to be allocated are lumped together and charged to cost centres on some predetermined ratio of unit activity to total company or group activity. The bases used more commonly are total expenses; payroll; cost of sales; sales; cost of investment or return on investment.

Individual Method:
> Where each category of expense to be allocated is charged out on an individual basis.
> The bases used include data processing to number of computer hours; legal expenses to direct staff hours and personnel department expenses to the recipient unit employee numbers.

Combination Method:
> Where certain identifiable expenses are charged out to cost centres on an individual basis; the remaining expenses distributed on the blanket basis.

Advantages and Disadvantages

Blanket Method:
> Relatively simple to administer
> Avoids distortions in charge out
> Easily understood
> Encourages economies in charge out base e.g. capital employed
> Charge out bears little relationship to service performed
> Charge out is arbitrary

Individual Method:
> Correspond more closely to actual services provided
> Less emotive to managers
> Overspending can be related to individual's responsibility
> Considerable administrative effort involved
> Charge outs give an impression of accuracy

Combination Method:
> Permits allocation of costs on a more identifiable basis
> More closely represents the actual situation;
> Imparts feeling of fairness
> Necessitates greater administrative and accounting effort

Guidelines relating to any cost allocation formula:

> the allocation basis must be seen to be effective and equitable;
> managers must be aware of the formula used;
> managers must be encouraged to question allocated costs;
> managers must be encouraged to reduce allocated cost by effectively altering the base under their control e.g. numbers employed;
> the allocation must be adhered to in such a manner as will influence decision-taking.

Marginal costing v. absorption costing.

Advantages of marginal costs procedures:

marginal costing systems are simple to operate, they do not involve the problems of overhead apportionments and recovery

marginal costing avoids the difficulties of having to explain the purpose and basis of overhead absorption. Fluctuations in profit are easier to explain because they result from cost-volume interactions and not from changes in inventory

marginal costing introduces a direct relationship between sales volume and marginal income (i.e. the contribution).

marginal costing shows which products are making a contribution and which are failing to cover their avoidable (i.e. variable) costs

Disadvantages of marginal costs procedures:

economic selling prices over the long run cannot be set without some attention being paid to fixed costs. Each product line/job must not just cover its marginal costs, but collectively the contributions of all jobs must cover at least all costs if a profit is to be made

the importance of time tends to be overlooked in marginal costing: two jobs may have the same marginal cost, but one may take twice as long to complete as the other and hence its 'true' cost will be more.

the difficulties and dangers of spreading fixed overhead costs do not mean that they should be ignored: they are just as vital as are direct wage costs, etc. in fact, as production becomes more automated and greater in volume, more costs will tend to be fixed, and hence they should not be overlooked

Factors which will determine the use of absorption costing or marginal costing will be:

the system of financial control in use (e.g. responsibility accounting is inconsistent with absorption costing).

the production methods in use (e.g. marginal costing is favoured in simple processing situations in which all products receive similar attention; but when different products receive widely differing amounts of attention, then absorption costing may be more realistic).

the significance of the prevailing level of fixed overhead costs.

A system of marginal costing should detect:

a change in either the selling price of a product or its variable cost rate will alter the break-even point and the contribution margin ratio (i.e. the proportion of sales revenue that is left when variable cost is deducted).

when sales are above the break-even point, a high contribution margin ratio will result in greater profits than will a small contribution margin ratio.

a low contribution margin ratio will require a large increase in sales volume to create a significant increase in profit.

if other factors stay constant, a change in total fixed costs will alter the break-even point by the same percentage and the net profit will vary by the same amount as the change in total fixed costs

7.30 FLOW OF MANUFACTURING COSTS IN VARIABLE COSTING

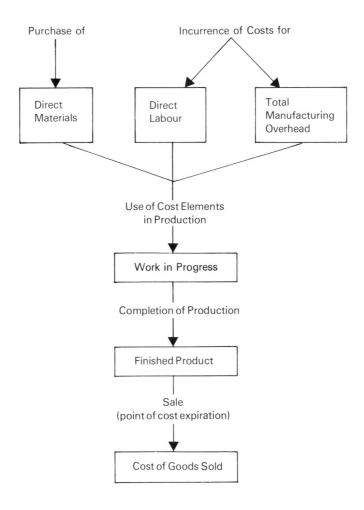

Purchase of

Incurrence of Costs for

Direct Materials

Direct Labour

Total Manufacturing Overhead

Use of Cost Elements in Production

Work in Progress

Completion of Production

Finished Product

Sale
(point of cost expiration)

Cost of Goods Sold

Is the company's costing system tailored to the company's needs?

Have cost centres been clearly defined?

Are the benefits of the system commensurate with its costs?

Are all costs classified into their direct and indirect, fixed and variable, controllable and uncontrollable, and separate and joint categories?

Is the behaviour of different costs understood in relation to changes in the level of activity?

Are cost reports made available promptly? How often? How quickly?

Could statements be presented earlier if more estimates were used? (Are estimating procedures reliable?)

Are figures rounded so that results are more easily understood?

Can any figures of small value be grouped?

Are the descriptions of reported items clear?

Are unusual items adequately explained?

W ill further (or less) mechanisation affect the overhead of cost accounting?

Can the effectiveness of cost accounting procedures be improved?

Has sufficient thought been given to the type of costing system to use? (for example, standard costing, absorption costing, or marginal costing.)

Has the purpose for which costing is being performed been fully considered? (for example, pricing, product costing, cost control)

Is the costing system adequate in determining the relative efficiencies and profitable divisions, processes, product lines, jobs?

Is the costing system adequate for the needs of EDP and operations research analysts?

Are ratios, graphs etc, used to supplement the figures produced by the costing system?

Is a satisfactory procedure being operated to price material issues from stores?

Are all withdrawals of stock and ordering of goods form outside suppliers duly authorised by requisitions?

Are job allocation numbers recorded against labour time, material usage, etc., in all cases?

Do employees understand the importance of recording the allocation of time to jobs? How are they encouraged to do this accurately?

What is the basis for the apportionment of each service departments' costs? Is the most suitable basis selected in every case?

How are overheads absorbed into productive output? Is the most suitable basis used?

What action is taken on the basis of over or under-recovery of overheads?

Are normalised over recovery rates used? If not, why not? For example, is the level of activity stable from month to month?

Have separate overhead rates been developed for fixed overhead costs and variable overhead costs?

Why are overheads absorbed (if they are absorbed)?

Is the contribution margin concept understood within the company?

Is cost-volume-profit analysis undertaken?

Is marginal costing undertaken?

Has the company's margin of safety ever been worked out?

Are the comparative advantages and disadvantages of marginal costing versus absorption costing fully appreciated?

Is the costing system closely geared to the type of production processes operated?

What role does cost accounting play in relation to special decision-making?

Does the cost control system have the active backing of top management?

Do controls conform to the organisation structures?

Is the system seen as being an essential part of the company's management process?

Are responsible individuals aware of the need to plan their activities?

Do those individuals charged with various costs really have control over these costs?

Are cost controls established according to the nature of the tasks?

Do all who require it receive cost information?

Do responsible individuals who are held accountable play a full role in setting cost levels?

Is cost control information geared to the requirements of responsible individuals?

Is the costing system adequate in general terms?

Do control reports cover both financial and related causal factors?

Are cost control requirements and reports discussed with recipients?

Does the basis of measuring desired performance reflect those aspects of output and input that are important?

Is the principle of management by exception followed?

Are results measured in accordance with the same units of measure in which the standards are set?

Do recipients of control information know how to extract the most essential facts?

Are controls flexible and economical in operation?

Are deviations reported rapidly?

Do controls help to explain variances and to indicate the corrective action that is required?

Are control reports brief, simple to read, and relevant?

Are actions taken on the basis of these reports?

Are control reports used to indicate relative efficiencies?

Do all employees understand the cost implications of their work?

Do all employees have cost targets?

Do the benefits of the cost control system outweigh its costs?

Are unnecessary reports eliminated, and are new ones introduced only when clearly needed?

Is the control system revised each time an organisational change takes place?

Do good relations exist between the accounting staff and line management?

Definition:

Break-even analysis is a technique which, by means of graphic representation, endeavours to indicate clearly the relationship between a company's costs, turnover and profit.

Fields of Application:

This analysis can be applied to nearly all commercial managerial problems, such as:—

What are the consequences of an intended price increase?
What are the consequences if the sales-mix is changed?
What are the consequences for the profit if the fixed and variable costs change?
At which level of turnover does the company begin to lose?
By how much can the turnover decrease before the company begins to lose?

Description:

Break-even analysis is based on cost and turnover information. This information is set out graphically. The division of the costs into fixed and variable costs is of essential importance. Fixed costs are ones which, over a set period, are not affected by any change in turnover (per unit sales); variable costs, on the other hand, are affected by the level of turnover.

Examples of fixed costs are:

Depreciation
Rent and rates
Heating (standing charge)
Telephone rentals
Fixed loan interest
Vehicle license
Certain insurance premiums
Administrative salaries

BREAK-EVEN CHART

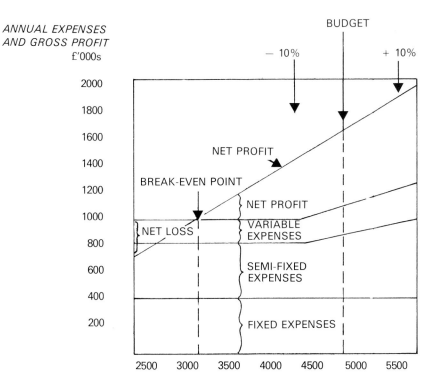

ANNUAL EXPENSES
AND GROSS PROFIT
£'000s

TURNOVER - £'000s

Interpretation:

	Budget turnover (less 10%) £000's	Budget £000's	Budget turnover (plus 10%) £000s
Turnover	4366	4852	5337
Gross Margin	1445	1667	1867
Fixed Expenditure	400	400	400
Semi Fixed Expenditure	434	500	560
Variable Expenditure	235	263	288
Total Expenditure	1049	1163	1248
Net Profit	396	502	619

Profit is earned when the cash equivalent is received from the buyer. A business has many income-producing activities operating at the same time and profit or loss from any one transaction is not readily identifiable. The following example shows the time cycle for one transaction from the commencement of manufacture until the profit is realised in cash.

The example also shows how credit terms given by raw material suppliers (including manual services) and that given to purchasers of the finished article affects the overall financing of the manufacturing process to the final sale and realisation of profit

Assumptions:

CREDITORS	TOTAL COST	PRODUCTION PROCESS	WEEKLY COST	CREDIT TERMS
Raw Material	£600	8 weeks	£75	5 weeks
Wages	£200	''	£25	2 weeks (i.e. paid at end of 2nd week)
Overheads	£120	''	£15	2 weeks
Cost of manufacture	£920		£115	
DEBTORS				
Selling Price	£1,000	—	—	2 weeks

Week	Cumulative Cost of Production		Amounts owed to Creditors	Bank Account			
				Weekly Cash		Cumulative Cash	
	Wkly. £	Cum. £	Cum. £	Rec'd £	Paid £	in credit £	overdrawn £
1	115	115	115		—		—
2	115	230	190		40		40
3	115	345	265		40		80
4	115	460	340		40		120
5	115	575	415		40		160
6	115	690	415		115		275
7	115	805	415		115		390
8	115	920	415		115		505
9		920	300		115		620
10		920	225		75		695
11			150	1000	75	230	
12			75		75	155	
13					75	80	

NOTES
1. The cost of production arises evenly over period of 8 weeks to £920. Until the article is sold and paid for the £920 has to be financed.
2. The amount available from creditors (including the week 1 wages in hand) rises to a maximum of £415. This is equivalent to an interest free loan.
3. Bank overdraft rises over the period as creditors are paid. If the buyer did not pay the £1.000 until week 14 the bank overdraft would rise to £920. No allowance has been made in the example for bank interest.
4. Time span is 11 weeks from commencement of production until profit received. After paying remaining creditors final cash balance at week 13 equals profit. The same information presented graphically would be:

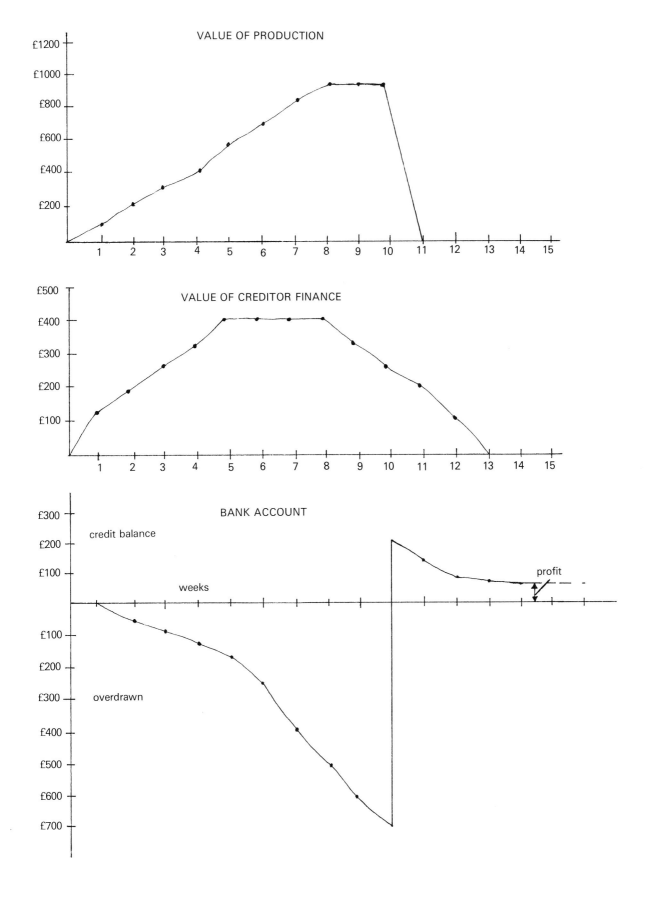

7.35 CASH MANAGEMENT

The management of cash is a vital part of every business activity — holding too few assets in the form of cash, or near cash, runs the risk of technical insolvency; holding too much, it is probably losing opportunities to earn additional revenue, thus making the whole enterprise more profitable.

Cash is both:
> an essential raw material
> a major product

Inflation has the following effects upon business:
> Increased values of credit sales require greater investment in debtors
> Markets are distorted, forcing companies to become more flexible in their operations
> Expenses rise faster than does the income from sales
> Traditional (historical cost) accounting does not show a true picture of a factual situation
> Product costing becomes difficult because of uncertainty in raw material costs
> Credit from suppliers becomes more difficult to obtain
> Suppliers pursue outstanding debts harder
> The value of stocks increases with no increase in volume sales
> Cost of new equipment escalates beyond the depreciation retention
> Loans become expensive and difficult to obtain unless backed by security

Trading in an inflationary economy means that more money is required to finance a business which has not changed the physical volume of its operations.

7.36 WORKING CAPITAL

The capital invested in items required to support expenses prior to their re-conversion into cash after the sale of a finished product or service is termed working capital.

Working capital is circulating capital

Working capital is the investment in:—
> Trade debtors (the amount owing by credit customers)
>
> Stock and work-in-progress

and financed by:
> Trade creditors (the amount owed to suppliers of materials)
>
> Bank overdrafts and short term loans

The aim is to:
> *minimise* the investment in debtors and stock and work-in-progress (ie current assets) and
> *maximise* the amounts owing to creditors and other short term lenders of capital (eg bank overdrafts (ie Current liabilities)

Achieve this aim in the case of:
> Debtors:—
> Ascertain financial credibility of customers
>
> Give minimum credit period
>
> Permit minimum credit outstanding beyond credit period
>
> Monitor collection procedure
>
> Stock:—
> Decide minimum stock levels
>
> Monitor stock usage and recording procedures
>
> Dispose of obsolescent stock quickly
>
> Creditors:—
> Establish rules for opening supplier accounts
>
> Check order procedure
>
> Negotiate maximum credit
>
> Negotiate longest credit period

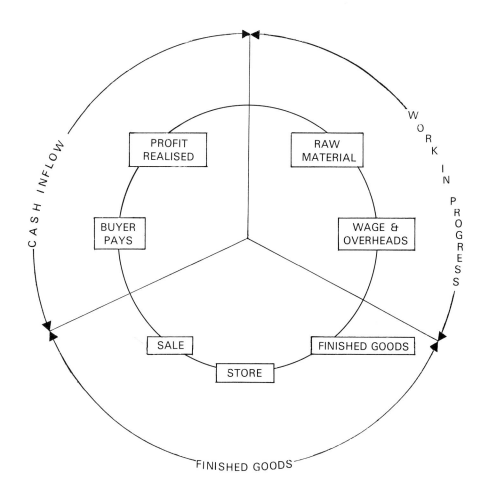

The above illustrates the cycle for manufacture of a single product. In reality the company is engaged in a series of manufacturing processes both of different articles and time spans, for example:

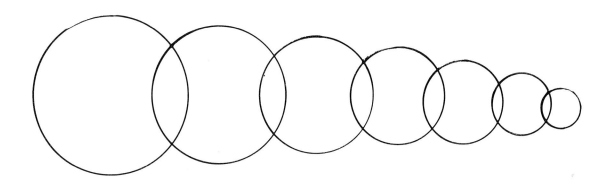

7.38 ACTION TO IMPROVE CASH FLOW CYCLE

Strategic:
>   operate more quickly
>   increase individuals responsibility
>   overhaul the information system
>   encourage management participation at all levels

Tactical:
>   manage business to maximise cash flow in short term
>   introduce more effective cash control systems
>   attempt larger and more effective cash forecasting techniques

Immediate Aims:
>   **speed up cash flows**
>   delay cash outflows
>   minimise delays in clearing funds to central bank
>   sell to third parties rather than internal customers
>   buy from other group companies where possible
>   **establish departmental or company targets** for cash reduction exercise
>   do not recruit staff except for vital tasks
>   consider staff utilisation generally
>   review minimum stock levels
>   determine total stock levels
>   analyse slow moving stock
>   convert redundant stock into cash
>   ensure maximum credit terms obtained from suppliers
>   curtail unnecessary capital expenditure
>   delay unnecessary revenue expenditure where no safety or health hazard is involved
>   keep debtor investment to minimum
>   consider 'cash with order' for new customers
>   set off debtor and creditor accounts where possible

7.39 OVERTRADING

'Overtrading' is trading in a way which results in proprietors or shareholders' investment no longer carrying all the risks.

If the net cash flow is insufficient to pay creditors, fixed assets might have to be sold to raise the money. This may mean the end of that business as a going concern.

Overtrading through ignorance or incompetence leads to financial resources being over-strained. This may show itself in over-investment in fixed assets, excessive credit being given or taken, the production cycle taking too long, inadequate planning of marketing and selling and an ineffective response to competitors (causing falling sales and lower margins).

Overtrading deliberately is all too often an unavoidable financial tactic (in the early stages) for a company wishing to expand fast and take full advantage of the opportunities open to it. In some cases, though, it comes as a considerable surprise when record profits are accompanied by a cash shortage. This arises through profits being confused with cash. They are, of course, entirely separate. Finance is about cash, and cash is normally required to support growth and higher profits — not vice versa. In rectifying the subsequent illiquidity, there are three points to take into account:

Sufficient time must be allowed to seek out and negotiate the appropriate new capital. This may take up to four months. If insufficient time is allowed, acute financial pressure can put the management in a weak bargaining position. Quite apart from this, financial institutions dislike being rushed and faced with emergencies; such an environment can make them very nervous and disinclined to invest.

The management must be able to demonstrate financial competence.

Running out of money is a sign of bad management and no financial institution called in at this stage will blithely disregard the warnings.

Analysis of the financing potential should disclose the following:

Present financial position — and its financing potential.

Net amount of new money required each year.

New assets requiring finance and whether or not they are suitable for money-raising.

What cushion required — how the inherent fund-raising capacity of various assets can be initially under-utilised to provide for this contingency in the future.

Proportion (gearing) of finance to be provided by the shareholders and other lenders (long, medium and short-term).

Cash which will become available to meet loan repayment obligations.

Level of net current assets.

Terms of credit granted by suppliers.

Credit terms with customers and bad debt record.

Six financial situations:

There are six financial situations worth distinguishing:

Insolvency — Companies with few assets and excessive debts.

Overtrading — Companies with illiquid assets and immediate debts. In order to survive, bills must be paid, other short-term commitments reduced and liquidity improved.

Expanding — Companies with assets and plans requiring funds for growth.

Worker/Shareholders requiring release of capital in a Non-Public Company

Budding entrepreneurs — Individuals with an idea but insufficient capital of their own.

Inflationary — Stable companies requiring finance to keep going.

Once the financial situation can be broadly classified, likely sources of finance can be identified.

A company seeking finance should know the following:

Purpose.

Amount required and planned/possible period of repayment.

Likely sources.

Facts supporting the request.

Long-term objectives based on commercially sound judgments.

An application for finance should include:

Estimate of the finance required to meet the company's operating plans.

Substantiation of the expected profits.

Forecast of the funds available internally and the external requirements.

Estimated timing for injection and repayment of borrowed funds. These should be separated into long, medium and short-term requirements, and so distinguished in the cash flow forecasts and projected sources and uses of funds statements. In preparing these figures, the business must be thought of in terms of cash not profits.

Four financial documents are required in support:

The opening (actual) and projected balance sheets throughout the relevant period.

Summarised projected trading accounts for that period.

Cash flow forecasts supporting the balance sheets and profit and loss accounts

Previous audited accounts

Prior to seeking finance, a case, containing certain information must be prepared to include:

Description of firm, history of achievements.
Description of management structure and senior management.
Summary of previous five years financial data (if available)
Copy of most recent audited accounts ideally along with relevant management accounts, control and monitoring procedures .
Summary of major influences on the profits and cash flow.
Summary of technical ability.
Summary by product classifications and order book.
Detailed projections for period covered by new financial requirements together with basic assumptions on which projections prepared. A note of the downside and upside risks is always helpful.
Amount of finance required, repayment schedule and security offered (if any).

Borrowers must NOT:

Procrastinate over repayment.
Fail to honour credit arrangements.
Gamble a way out of trouble.

Responsibilities of Insurance Manager:

Identification of risks and recommendations
Appropriate cover
Maintaining insurance covers.
Making recommendations on risk improvement.
Handling claims.
Maintaining communications within company and with external insurers and advisors.
Maintaining adequate records.
Maintaining constant review of company policy regarding levels and types of cover
Ensuring Insurance Manual is kept up-to-date.

Insurance Manual — contents:

Corporate policy on insurance.
Responsibility for insurance matters.
Brief description of insurance covers
Procedure for communicating catastrophy or other accident.
Procedure for claim notification and settlement.
Personnel policies affecting employee insurance.
Valuation procedures, professional advisors and incorporation of revised valuations.
Maintenance of fire fighting and prevention equipment.
Protection of records.

Advantages of insurance brokers:

Wide knowledge of insurance market.
Specialised knowledge and expertise.
Access to all insurance markets.
Prestige as intermediaries.
Assistance in negotiating premium rates and the settlement of claims.
Independent surveying services.
Worldwide representation.

How strong is the product range of Company X?

Are competitors likely to become more effective in the near future?

Are the markets for the products of Company X growing or declining? How and why?

Will Company X still be successful for the foreseeable future?

Stages in acquisition:

Exploration   Proposition
Screening   Negotiation
Investigation   Integration

Key pitfalls:

Failing to place responsibility at a sufficiently high level

Failing to establish a real unanimity of opinion as to what the acquisition objectives should be

Setting unrealistic criteria for today's competitive sellers' market

Searching only among companies for sale

Failing to recognise the time required for a successful acquisition programme

Failing to focus the search correctly

Failing to investigate prior to actual negotiations

Failing to assess correctly a seller's motives

Overlooking opportunities by using mechanical screening procedures

Failure to obtain qualified outside assistance when needed

Too much analysis and too little action; or vice versa.

For a successful acquisition programme:

Establish clearly defined growth objectives.

Establish acquisition criteria

Establish highly creative effort with appropriate supervision

Note: Improved control of early stages of programme will result in significant savings in time and money.

Special considerations:

The objectives of a merger must be defined in advance before the assessment takes place. A plan in relation to the organisation, management, marketing and manufacturing policies of the merged company must be known or prepared in the course of the appraisal, to avoid misunderstanding about what is intended and how it is to be achieved.

The management style of the two companies must be explored and compared.

Potential leaders of the combined management team must be identified.

Merger checklist:

What is the acquisition strategy of the company initiating the merger?

Does the company being appraised fit the defined specification?

Does it fit the parent?

Does the management style of the two companies fit?

Is there enough management talent?

Is the merger to eliminate product competition or simplify the combined product range?

Is a monoply situation created and if so what conditions must be satisfied?

To what extent will rationalisation of production facilities be possible?

Can a saving be achieved in administration overheads?

Is the position relating to raw material supplies strengthened?

Does the combined organisation attract greater purchasing power?

What is the effect of the merger on the trading operations situated abroad?

Are there any political conditions to be satisfied in the overseas territories?

What financing arrangements are necessary prior to and subsequent to the merger?

What Stock Exchange requirements must be fulfilled?

Have profit forecasts been made for the combined company?

What is the benefit to the ultimate shareholders in terms of earnings per share?

Index